FLYING NAKED 2

THE HUNT FOR VILCABAMBA'S GOLD

MICHAEL BLERIOT

MACGREGOR BOOKS

ALSO BY MICHAEL BLERIOT

Flying Naked – An American Pilot in the Amazon Jungle
Flying Naked 2 – The Hunt for Vilcabamba's Gold
The Jungle Express
Wings of Blue
Memories of an Emerald World

Under the name D. M. Sears:

Bad Day in the Late Wisconsin

The Untimely Journey of Veronica T. Boone series
Book 1 - Laurentide
Book 2 - The Jeremy Bentham
Book 3 - The White City

Copyright © 2015 D.M. Sears

All rights reserved.

No part of this book may be reproduced in any manner whatsoever without written permission except in the case of brief quotations embodied in critical articles or reviews.

Cover art by 100 Covers

ISBN: 0-9833751-8-6

ISBN-13: 978-0-9833751-8-0

*To the Pilots, Crews, and Mechanics
of the C-27*

Contents

Forward	IX
Map of the flying area	XII
1. Quito	1
2. Evan	38
3. Spies, flies, and shrunken heads	49
4. Maximón	117
5. Kids	145
6. Vilcabamba	172
7. Fin	228
The List	237
Glossary	239
About the Author	241

Forward

This volume is the follow-on and conclusion to *Flying Naked: An American Pilot in the Amazon Jungle*. Like that book and the three that preceded it (*Memories of an Emerald World*, *The Jungle Express*, and *Wings of Blue*), this book is about a plane.

To be precise, the books are about a plane, the jungle, and the guys who flew the plane into the jungle. The C-27A Spartan was a twin-engine turboprop transport aircraft used by the U.S. military in Central and South America during the 1990s. It was large enough to carry several tons of cargo and people but small enough to get into most of the airstrips scattered around the jungles of the region. Pilots and crews flew into the jungle to supply locations too remote for helicopters to reach and too small for bigger aircraft to land.

The stories in these books are also an attempt to capture what it was like to live in Panama during the waning days of the Canal Zone. If you've ever been in the military, regardless of the service, you know there are some locations the government can send you that are lousy, some that are okay, and some that you remember for the rest of your life as a great adventure. Panama was one of those great adventure places.

The C-27 had one home, Howard Air Base in Panama. Crews also staged temporary operations from satellite fields in Honduras and Peru. From these locations they reached sites as far north as

Guatemala and as far south as Bolivia, from the Pacific coast to the Brazilian Amazon.

The C-27 fleet and the U.S. military left Panama in 1999 when the United States gave the Canal Zone and everything in it to the country of Panama.

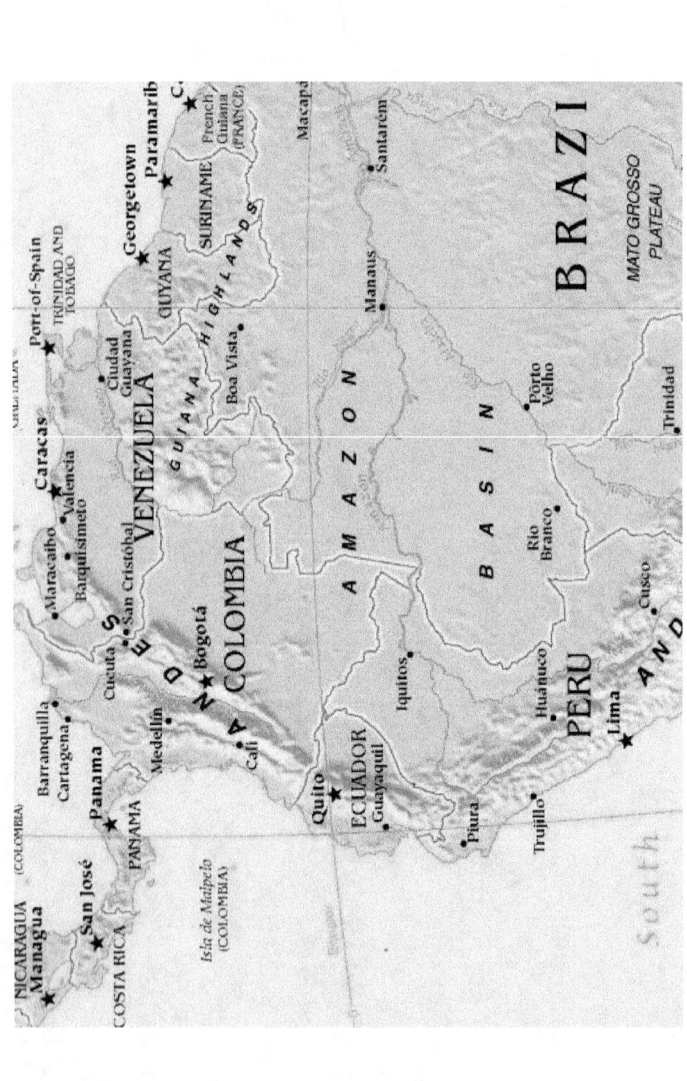

1

Quito

Walt talked the squadron into sending me to a language school in Quito, Ecuador. It wasn't easy since the Air Force had already sent me to a school in Guatemala. It made no sense for them to spend more money if I hadn't learned enough Spanish the first time.

But Walt convinced Major Farnham that a lull in the ops tempo was coming up and that perhaps a compromise was in order. To wit: Farnham would give me the time off but I would have to pay for the trip myself. Since the school in Quito was only nine dollars a day, this was a bargain.

"I'm surprised," I told Walt after buying my tickets. "I didn't expect the chief scheduler would be willing to lose a pilot for a month."

"Pure self interest," he replied.

"How so?"

"Ecuador is ground zero for our treasure hunt. Take the list with you."

I patted my breast pocket which held the list we all carried. "What in particular? Which one?"

Walt crossed his feet on his desk and put his hands behind his head. "Doesn't matter," he said. "You'll think of something."

***

I arrived in Quito late on a Saturday night. The school sent a driver to pick me up and deliver me to a local family who had agreed to host me for a month. Their house, and their neighborhood, and in fact much of the airport where my plane landed was enduring a nightly rolling blackout due to electricity shortages so it took the driver a while to find his way. When we finally found the house, all I could see was a shadowy structure and a tiny front lawn.

"*Beinvenidos*," said a small voice at the front door. It belonged to a middle-aged lady with a bright smile. "*Bienvenidos al Ecuador!*"

***

She stepped aside and motioned for me to enter the house. The doorway was narrow and in the dark I tripped over the threshold and fell backward over my own suitcase, tumbling through the foyer and into the living room. The only thing hurt was my pride but the injury compounded when I learned Señora Lidy Digard wasn't alone.

Five young women sat on couches along the wall. Candles burned on the table between them, the leaping flames throwing shadows as thought it was a coven of witches. Unlike witches, the women didn't cackle. Instead, they gasped as I made my entrance, falling as though dropped from the roof. When they saw I was unhurt they collapsed into giggling.

Welcome to Ecuador, indeed.

"*Buenas noches*," I said from the floor.

The tallest girl was Karla, Lidy's daughter. "We've been waiting for you," she said.

I looked around the room, wondering what she meant. "Do you *all* live here?" I asked. My enthusiasm must have been obvious because they broke into laughter again.

"No, pobrecito! Solamente en tus sueños!"

My dreams aside, this was still better than the house full of children that I had endured in Guatemala.

"*Bueno*," Señora Digard interrupted, bustling around with an excitement that was flattering. "Let's get you to your room. You must be tired."

"*Pero, mamá!*" implored Karla. "We're going out."

"Maybe he doesn't want to go out. He has been traveling."

"*Gracias, señora*," I said to Lidy. "Thank you for letting me stay here in your home. I'm looking forward to my time in Quito."

She held her candle high and waved for me to follow.

"We have a room for you in the back. Let me show you."

Karla grabbed my arm as her mother went down the hall.

"We are going to a club," she whispered. "We waited for you. Do you want to go?"

I looked at their five expectant faces. "Go to a club with five beautiful women? I think I can do that."

"*Vaya!*" they shrieked, and pushed me down the hallway. "Then hurry!"

***

Sandy, one of Karla's friends, drove us downtown, all six of us crammed into her Toyota Corolla. The girls never stopped talking.

The roads in Ecuador were in horrible shape. Sandy swerved regularly and with no warning to avoid both pedestrians and potholes, violent moves that had me and Karla and two of her friends hanging onto each other in the back seat – a not unpleasant experience.

The drive was also exciting because of the view. Quito is at 9,000 feet above sea level and built in a depression between volcanoes. So many rifts spread through the city in so many fault lines that it's hard to drive a direct route between two locations. And because the city dips toward the middle, anyone on the east side can see all the way across to the west side. That was how we drove in that night, skirting the Pichincha volcano and looking down as the lights in one corner of the city after another faded out, disappearing in strings and swathes while lights somewhere else blazed into existence as the rolling blackout continued .

"This area is called New Town," Karla announce when we drove into a still-lighted area along Avenida 12 de Octubre. "There are clubs here." The girls shouted suggestions to Sandy as she picked her way through traffic.

We found a cafe instead of a club. The girls wanted to meet their new visitor more than they wanted to dance or drink, so we parked and ducked into a place where the walls were covered with a mural of the Mitad del Mundo, the site north of Quito that marked the official line of the equator. Large yellow suns spotted the ceiling.

"Pues, díganos, Miguel," Sandy began the quizzing after we ordered food. *"Que haces aquí?"*

"What am I doing here?" I repeated. "What do you mean?"

"Why are you here in Ecuador?"

"Why, to study Spanish."

"Pero, ya hablas espanol. Tu hablas bien!"

"No, *chicas*. I need more practice."

"Bueno, we can give you practice," she insisted. "It is sooo boring here. Now that you are here we can do things exciting!"

"Like what?" I asked.

"I don't know! But something. We must take you somewhere."

"Well," I agreed. "I have always wanted to see Ecuador. I fly over it all the time."

Karla sighed happily. "*Sí, eres piloto*. Now I know a pilot."

"She likes to meet people who are different," Sandy explained.

"I do not have the money to travel," Karla explained, showing no bitterness. "So I meet people. The more people I meet, the more *different* people, the more the world comes to me. It is my way of traveling!"

"I like that," I told her. "You'll learn all about the world."

"But you, Miguel, where do you want to go in Ecuador?"

"Well," I mused, "I go to the jungle but I've not had a chance to see the mountains. The lakes, the volcanoes – they're beautiful."

"*Sí!*"

"And Quito...what an amazing city!"

Their fervor ebbed. Karla had trouble seeing how I could be excited about sticking around in the capital.

"Tell us about where you are from," they insisted.

I told them about Chicago.

"Chicago? Michael Jordan, yes?" inquired Maria Vicente, one of the friends. She was tall and thin with almost-blonde hair.

"*Sí.*"

"And gangsters," her cousin Alma offered. "Al Capone?"

"Uh, yes. But that was a while ago."

"What countries have you visited?" Antonita, the last girl, wanted to know. She was a visitor herself, a friend from Chile. "How many countries have you traveled to?"

The girls leaned forward. I hesitated. They were interested in me because I was a foreigner who represented things they had heard of but not seen. At the same time, if I came right out and told them I had been to 40-some countries it would sound arrogant. The unspoken message would be that their country was just another dot on the map.

"Not many," I begged off. "I just go where the military sends me."

"But where?" they insisted.

I relented and told them about trips I had made to Egypt while flying the big C-5 Galaxy, the plane I had started my career in and the one I hated. I emphasized that I was in Egypt to support humanitarian efforts in Africa.

"And the pyramids? You saw the pyramids?"

I described my trips to the pyramids, leaving out the detail of staying in a five-star hotel only a mile away. They pressed for more, wanting to know about the Egyptians, their cars, their stores, the sand, and the Nile River. They kept me talking until I felt like I had relived my months on the ground there.

"And where else?" Alma demanded. "Where else have you gone?"

I mentioned England, Germany, and Italy.

"Ah, Italia!..." they swooned and begged for every detail of those trips.

The waitress brought us a plate of yucca and bottles of soda. The girls quizzed me until long after the meal was over. At last I got the question I was expecting.

"Pues, Miguel," Karla wanted to know. "Of all the countries you have visited, what is your favorite?"

"Bueno, Ecuador, por supuesto!"

"Oooohhhhhhh..."

"Miguel," Karla confronted me. "Ecuador cannot be your favorite country. We are small, we are poor, we have nothing here. Even with the mountains. We have no pyramids. We do not have *el Vaticano* or great fashion. We are not important."

Her look was dismissive. Her friends, too, gave thin smiles and looked about as though wishing to change the subject. I was shocked. I couldn't remember ever meeting someone who didn't have good things to say about their country. Without thinking, I disagreed with her.

"*Chica loca*. Crazy girl. You are wrong."

"*No.*"

"*Sí*. I will prove it to you. Tell me about your country."

"*Cómo?*"

"Tell me about your country," I insisted. "I know nothing of Ecuador except what I told you. Tell me about the mountains. Tell me about your government." I turned to Sandy and the others. "Tell me about your schools. Tell me where you work and what you do and how big is your family. Tell me about the buses and the taxis and how much it costs to buy a car. *Dígame*, how do you travel from here to the coast? Where do tourists go and where do *you* wish they would go? Tell me everything."

"Miguel, there is nothing..."

"Tell me about dating."

"*Cómo?*"

"*Sí!* Tell me about the boys you date. What movies do you go to? What are you favorite TV shows? Come on, *dígame*!"

With the tables turned, they started talking.

"Everyone votes?" I interrupted at one point.

"*Sí*," Sandy answered as though it was the most natural thing in the world. "When there is an election, everyone must vote. If you do not, you cannot get a driver's license, you cannot get a marriage license, you cannot collect unemployment benefits. We have 100% participation in every election." She paused for a moment, realizing something. "We are a better democracy than your United States!"

I held my tongue. Ecuador had had 40 elected presidents and 50 dictators in its 180 years of existence. The measure of a democracy, I wondered, might be found in the quality of its voters rather than its quantity.

"True," I conceded carefully, "that's more than we do in the States."

They talked about the bus system and argued amongst themselves over the best way for me to get to my school. They took sides over which volcano near the capital was the prettiest. They bopped from one topic to the next as each girl tried to find something different about their country to brag about.

"We have the only glacier on the equator," Maria Vicente piped up. "On Mount Cotopaxi."

"Oh?"

"And we produce more bananas than any other country," Karla said proudly. "And more varieties: baby banana, red banana, yellow banana, cooking banana, Cavendish banana,..."

"And we make Panama hats," Sandy interrupted. "Not Panama."

"And you are at the middle of the world," I reminded her, pointing to the mural.

"*Sí.*"

"*Y la selva,*" I added. "*Uds. tienen la selva.*"

Sí, they conceded. The jungle was nice. That got them talking about the jungle and then about oil which had been discovered there. Oil started them talking about the economy which brought up tourism. Tourism reminded them of their beaches which caused Sandy to remember a story about green sea turtles surfacing on a beach near Galera and scaring a family of French visitors. And the mention of turtles reminded them of the Galapagos...

"Aaiiee!" they shrieked in unison. "*Las islas Galapagos!*"

None of them had been there but they knew about the islands. So confidently did Sandy tell me about volcanoes and black sand beaches, and Karla talk about penguins and sea lions and giant tortoises, and Maria lecture me on how the islands were a national preserve that eventually I looked to Antonita for assistance.

"Help," I begged.

She laughed and shook her head. As a Chilean, she said, she was happy for her neighbors. They had an unequalled treasure off their shores.

The Ecuadorians beamed.

"*Pues*, you see," I told them. "You are a small country but that does not mean you have nothing. No one in the world – not even *Italia* – has everything that you have in Ecuador."

"*Sí, Miguel!*" they enthused. "And you must see it all while you are here! You must see it all!"

***

The Simon Bolivar School was a compact building on Avenida 6 de Diciembre. I signed up for three hours of language study per day.

On the roof was a garden of flower boxes that faculty and students used as a break area in between lessons. In the basement was a dance floor. Three days into my studies I wandered downstairs in response to a flyer for a free dance lesson. A dozen other students were already there, milling about.

"Are you here for the class?" the teacher asked me. I recognized her as Ana, one of the language instructors. She had the wispy frame of a ballet dancer and the smile of a nun.

"Yes," I answered. "I thought I'd try."

"Wonderful! We need more men."

Ten minutes later I understood why men were in short supply. The first dance Ana led us through was the cumbia, a hip-swiveling Latin dance that was foreign to my body. None of us took to it naturally. We linked up in awkward pairs and made jerky attempts to imitate Ana's moves.

Every few minutes we switched partners. Then Ana turned on the stereo.

"Con música!" she enthused. "It is easier to dance with the music."

"You look like you're in pain," the girl I was dancing with said to me. Her name was Lisa. She was short with cropped hair and sharp blue eyes that challenged me to lie.

"That's because I'm in pain," I admitted. "I don't dance well. This cumbia-thing is murder on my hips."

"I know what you mean." She watched her feet as though they were independent creatures. "I'm not doing this right."

"Are you in the school?" I asked.

"The language school? Yes."

"How is your host family?"

She tried to turn the way Ana demonstrated but ended up facing away from me. She turned back, confused.

"Nice. At least I think they're nice. I don't understand anything they say."

The music changed to a salsa. Ana showed us turns that were easier on the joints but that still required a fluidity I didn't feel.

I was comfortable leading turns though not always doing them myself. Even then I found that with an inexperienced dancer like Lisa I had to be careful. She stood only as high as my shoulder and had a light frame that was easy to spin off into space if I pushed too hard.

"Baila, baila!" Ana commanded and put on a faster song. We complied, trying to match the beat.

"How do you like Quito?" I asked, gamely keeping up the conversation so as to distract us both from our horrible dancing.

"I can't breathe," she answered.

"Because of the pollution or the altitude?"

"No, I mean I can't breathe right now. You're holding me too tight."

"Oh." I released her from a failed turn. "Sorry."

"Good," she continued, catching her breath. "It's good being here. I needed a break."

"From what? What do you do?"

"I'm a writer. I got a grant from a corporation and they said I could do anything with it. They probably intended that I use it to research my next project but I decided to travel."

"And you chose Ecuador?"

She shrugged. In combination with the sidestep she was doing it made her look like a vaudeville act. "It's cheap. And I never would have come here otherwise."

Ana taught us some cha-cha but then returned to the salsa before the class ended. It was the dance where the fewest students fell down.

"Es bonita!" she shouted as we swiveled around the room. "You are all doing very well!"

***

After that first night in New Town, Karla really wanted to impress me with her country. I liked Ecuador and told her so but she felt a need to show me that her nation was equal on every level with the United

States. That was a tougher sell. She guessed as much and watched for any signs of condescension in what I said or did.

That wasn't fair because even when I didn't feel superior she would infer it unless I reacted in just the right way. When the power failed in the middle of dinner, for example, which it did almost every night, it wasn't easy to carry on the conversation without at least making the observation that the house was now dark. But if I made such an observation Karla and her mother were immediately embarrassed. When she and I jumped on a *popular* bus one day to ride to the park I found the seats were too small for me to sit down – and the ceiling wasn't high enough for me to stand up. It was hard not to make a joke as we rumbled down the street with me hunched like Quasimodo in the aisle so I said to a little boy sitting nearby, "The stores never have clothes that fit me, either." The little boy laughed. Karla, on the other hand, took my comment as a slur on Quito's public transportation.

I tried to be careful. Whenever things like that happened I tried to keep quiet and maintain a blank stare. But occasionally I tripped and gave her real ammunition, as I did when we argued over the pollution.

Pollution on Quito's streets was horrible. Cars with no catalytic converters belched fumes thick enough to hide behind. If I made the mistake of standing on a busy corner when the traffic lights turned to green, I had to wait for the clouds of exhaust to clear before venturing across. That and the altitude made it a struggle for me to walk down a main street. Only three days into my visit I had a sore throat and a cough. When Karla asked why, I didn't stop to think and told her what I thought was the reason. She grew angry.

"*La contaminación* is no worse here than in the United States!" she retorted.

"Well," I tried to be diplomatic, "we have unleaded gas in the U.S. so that helps a little."

"No!" she informed me. "Your pollution is just as bad."

I had embarrassed her again, of course, which wasn't my intent. But then there was the bus incident, and then I got a case of food poisoning at a local cafe. I made light of all of it, insisting it could happen in any city in any country, but the look in her eyes told me she suspected I mocked Ecuador under my breath.

The first Sunday I was in town was the Fourth of July. That afternoon Sandy and Karla hustled me into the car and drove to a soccer field down the street from the American Embassy. It was a hot, dry day and a crowd gathered there in the nearest goal zone and on the hillside overlooking the pitch. Most of the people were locals but half a dozen Embassy employees stood around, too, wearing the bemused looks of people used to celebrating Yankee traditions in out of the way places.

The ambassador, a tall, taciturn man, stood in a collection of local dignitaries near the middle of the field. He held a plastic cup full of beer in one hand and with his other worked the crowd, a firm handshake or a pat on the back ready for all the aldermen and business leaders in attendance.

Neither the ambassador nor the businessmen paid attention to the neighborhood residents who gathered on the hill. The girls and I joined the crowd there, settling in halfway up the slope by pushing over the high grass that folded under us like a cushion.

"Are we waiting for something?" I asked.

"You'll see," Karla giggled.

"Is there going to be a soccer game?"

"No."

After a while a van pulled up. A man leaped out who everyone seemed to know. The people on the hill cheered: he waved. With the help of two others he removed a bamboo structure from his truck and carried it to the center of the dry, overgrown soccer field.

"Que es eso?" I asked the girls.

"Son fuegos artificiales!" Karla squealed, clapping her hands.

I looked closely. The structure was a wooden trellis folded into a column. It was flimsy, with great gaps, and was the kind of thing a bunch of Cub Scouts would have put together if they'd been told to build a replica of the Washington Monument and had only string and old wicker baskets to do it. It didn't even stand straight. Its builder had to fold a towel and place it under one of the tower's legs to keep it from falling over. The tower itself seemed aware of its precarious state. Red, white, and blue ribbons fluttered from every angle so that it appeared to shiver with anxiety when there was a breeze.

But sure enough, there were *fuegos artificiales*. The skeletal contraption was riddled with fireworks. They were tied on to every crosspiece, corner, and limb from ground level to the peak and stuck out like gun barrels from a paranoid fortress. A fuse linked them, beginning at the bottom and wrapping around and around the obelisk until climbing eight feet to the top and finishing at the *pièce de résistance*, a muffler-sized Chinese rocket that resembled something Wile E. Coyote might ride as he chased the Roadrunner.

"Hay muchos!" Karla and Sandy agreed, pointing out that last year the tower had been smaller and had fewer rockets.

An Ecuadorian man wearing a polo shirt and a cowboy hat got the attention of the crowd. Karla whispered to me that he was the leader of the local electoral parish. People cleared the pitch and clustered on the hill.

The man made a speech. Then the ambassador made a speech. When he finished the crowd clapped, yelled *Viva America!* and chanted for the van man to light the fuse.

"Normally, we watch fireworks at night," I commented to Sandy.

"*Sí,*" she agreed. "But here people go to bed early so we do it during the day."

The van man stepped forward with a lighter and knelt at the base of the tower. It must not have worked because after a while he asked if anyone had matches. An alderman stepped forward with a pack and the two of them discussed striking technique. Finally, Van Man struck one and held it to the fuse.

"Ahhhh..." the crowd enthused as a puff of smoke signaled that the fuse lighted. "Oooooo," they cooed as sparks leaped into view. Their enthusiasm was contagious – and endearing. How could I not like people who were excited by a sputtering fuse? Karla and Sandy clasped hands across my lap. Everyone on the hill leaned forward in anticipation. A hundred pairs of eyes followed the progress of the burning line as it moved across the column to the nearest firework.

Pow!

The explosion elicited cheers. It was just a firecracker but you would have thought we had heard a cannon blast. Our group on the hill broke into sustained applause.

Bang! Whoosh!

Another firecracker and then a bottle rocket. Then a third explosion that was bigger than the first two. The pyrotechnics were spaced out so each had a few seconds to entertain before its neighbor blasted into the air. And entertain they did. Even in broad daylight there was something exhilarating about a sudden blast or whoosh or line of smoke that raced across the sky so fast we couldn't follow the missile that left it. Each device was a surprise, too, for Van Man had decorated his launch pad with a variety of explosives. There were firecrackers, sparklers, and Roman candles; Chinese showers and zoomer rockets; Crazy Hedgehogs and Screaming Dragons and snakes and smoke bombs that draped the field in a multicolored fog. Through the haze we watched a pinwheel fly off the rack and spin its way ten feet into the air as it threw a spiral of sparks in every direction. Another close behind it spiraled the opposite direction so that for a second it looked as though the tower was waving two fiery arms in celebration.

Oohhhhhhh…aaahhhhhhhh.

As the fuse worked its way up the column the toys grew grander, the explosions deeper, the trails of fire longer. They weren't huge – none of the fireworks was anything more than what roadside stands sold under tents back home in Illinois. But here in our low-key gathering they became as exciting as anything the City of Chicago ever launched over Grant Park. I cheered.

Fwrrrrrrrrrrrrr.

It was when a third pinwheel launched itself off the flimsy scaffolding that a warning bell sounded in my mind. The fireworks were flying in every direction – up, laterally, some stayed fixed to the structure and spewed colored fire into the air. Sparks went with them and many drifted eagerly into the dry grass.

The first sign of trouble came after a dozen fireworks had gone off. A cherry-popper flew off a lower rack and instead of exploding in mid-air it landed in the far penalty box. The fan of sparks the explosion threw up started several small fires that the nearest spectators were obliged to stamp out when the flames didn't die but instead advanced toward a pair of toddlers in a wooden wagon at the base of the hill. People pitched in merrily, seeing it as part of the show.

They hadn't finished when a Roman candle erupted off the second deck with such force that it blew out of its holder and onto the pitch. There it fell over and shot fire into ten feet of grass that soon produced more smoke than the candle itself. Van Man even trotted over with a blanket to beat that one out. He was joined by one of the Americans who displayed commendable choreography as he stamped while shimmying between successive blasts from the relentless fuse behind him.

But it was a Patriot fountain, imprudently fixed on the lower half of the tower, that brought the activities to a climax. Knocked loose by the Roman candle, it leaned inward instead of toward the pitch and when lighted launched a shower of sparks straight up into dozens of other rockets waiting their turn. An entire side of the obelisk caught fire. Fireworks of all kinds began to detonate out of turn. With a look of horror Van Man raced to his creation, only to be driven back by a fusillade of bottle rockets that launched themselves across the field and made everyone dive for cover. The tower shook, leaned, and toppled.

It fell pointing toward the hill. The whole scaffold went up in flames and waves of mortars, star shells, and flares arced into the hayfield where we sat, causing a stampede as scores of people grabbed children and belongings and ran to escape the spreading flames.

Sandy disappeared somewhere. I took Karla by the hand and led her downhill, against the crowd, dodging missiles along the way but reasoning that now the soccer pitch itself was relatively safe. We worked our way behind the collapsed scaffolding and then watched the remaining fireworks explode against a backdrop of billowing smoke. The hillside was ablaze. Where we sat earlier turned to blackened ground in seconds as a wall of fire raced up to the street above. The charred wagon rested in the foreground, its former occupants being carried down the street by their still fleeing parents. The bangs and whistles of Independence Day mingled with their screams.

Karla watched the scene before her and bit her lip. I tried to make the best of it.

"It's a beautiful display," I insisted as the Roadrunner rocket finally launched and shot straight into the hillside. It stuck there like an unexploded bomb from our Air Force training films, then burst into a ball of blue and red flames that flickered long after the other fires went out. "You know, given the circumstances."

"Don't make fun," she said quietly.

"I'm not! Really, Karla, this is...this is something unique. Really, I'll remember it forever."

But my efforts were wasted. She began to cry.

***

The next week Karla announced that she and Sandy would take me to Otavalo, a town seventy miles north of Quito along the spine of the Andes.

"Why are we going there?" I asked.

"To shop," she replied.

We drove up late Friday after classes. For three hours Sandy's Corolla negotiated the Pan American Highway north along the Andean ridge in the fading afternoon light. The terrain was dry, with mountains on our left and cliffs plunging to valleys below on the right. As the sky darkened and the highway turned to gravel, it felt like we were traveling back in time.

***

In Otavalo we looked for a hotel the girls could afford since they wouldn't let me pay for them. It took a while. Almost every hotel, pension, and guest house was full due to Saturday being market day. Finally we found two rooms in a small building off Jaramillo Street that cost less than six dollars apiece.

For four dollars I got a room with a single bed. There were no dressers, chairs, tables, closets, or baths. There was no mirror. The toilets and showers were down the hall.

"It's good?" Sandy asked me when I met them again downstairs.

"Perfect," I insisted. Karla eyed me askance, alert for even a hint of insincerity.

It was quiet all night, the silence being more eerie for the fact that we knew the town was full of visitors wanting to shop in the market in the morning. The temperature dropped into the thirties. By midnight I was shivering beneath the thin blanket the hotel provided.

***

The next morning I learned that for four dollars there was no hot water, either. Since the building was unheated I took a lightning-fast shower and dressed as fast as possible. I was still shivering when Karla and Sandy met me outside. Karla pointed up the street.

"There are two markets," she explained. "One for animals, up there. The other is around the corner. We're going to show you the animals first, then go to the trade market for clothes. We have to get there early to get the best deals."

We walked three blocks, crossed a stream, and found an acre of trampled field coming to life in the early light. A small roundup was underway. Half a dozen livestock trucks backed up against a knoll overlooking the stream and used the slope of the hill to unload their animals. There were cows, pigs, goats, sheep, chickens, and llamas everywhere.

"Are we buying anything?" I asked my companions.

"Not unless you are going to ride it back to Quito," Sandy said firmly. "No pig is going in my car."

"*Venga*," Karla directed. "Now we will go to the *mercado artesania*."

The artisan market was in the square half a block from our hotel. The night before it had been empty; today its cobblestones were packed with tents and tables set up by Incan craftsman who scurried around in ponchos and fedoras. They had set up in the pre-dawn darkness and now looked as established as if they had always been there. Anything made of wool or leather was for sale.

"The best time to buy is now," Sandy counseled.

We wandered for hours. Most of the stalls sold the same collection of textiles: ponchos, jumpers, sweaters, capes, socks, hats, and blankets were stacked high in every direction, high enough that merchants used hooked poles to retrieve items. At each stall the girls lectured me on the different clothing, the fabrics, and how to talk the sellers into a good price. The sellers were well-versed in their art, too, however, and it wasn't long before I found myself the owner of a thick, hooded poncho.

"This is heavy wool," I observed, handling it and wondering when I would ever wear it in Panama.

"But soft," Karla pointed out. "See, it's alpaca. Alpaca is the softest wool you can get except for vicuña."

She reminded me of something. Vicuña was on Walt's list.

"Do they have vicuña?"

"Maybe," Sandy said. "But vicuña is very expensive. And rare. It's illegal unless the vendor has a government permit."

"Do you know anybody who might sell it?" I asked the vendor. He shook his head. I explained why I wanted vicuña but he offered an apologetic smile.

Karla and Sandy conversed. "Let's look," they insisted.

We split up and rambled for the rest of the morning. None of us had any luck. Everyone we met agreed on the merits of vicuña wool but nobody sold it. The problem was that not only were vicuña rare, they were wild. Vicuña lived at high altitudes – 12,000 to 16,000 feet – and didn't like it when they were brought to lower ground. They also didn't like being fenced in. Put them in a corral and they would jump over walls or batter on gates until free and then run like the wind. Attempts to breed them failed. Attempts to crossbreed them with the more docile alpaca succeeded but the resulting wool was lower quality. Since the animals can be shorn only once every three years and even then give up just a single pound of wool, most people found keeping the animals not worth while. That's why so few people did it and why clothing from the animal was like gold.

***

On one sweep of the market a woman tugged at my sleeve. She sold wildflowers and offered me a fresh bouquet of red and yellow asters. The sweet smell of honey and pollen and fresh mountain air rose up from her table.

Sandy appeared at the table and laughed when she saw me sniffing the flowers.

"You like flowers!" she giggled.

"I was testing them for you, my beautiful hostess," I smiled. "I came to get you a bouquet."

"*Ay, qué bonita!*" she interrupted, and pointed to a tiny vase of brilliant blue flowers at the back of the lady's stall. The petals were so blue and perfect they looked like a painting.

"*Sí,*" the woman nodded to the flowers proudly and held out the vase for us to look. The cuttings were like daisies but the petals were the richest shade of blue imaginable. Their rounded forms spread flat and clung to each other as though joined, encircling a delicate eye of almost the same hue. I picked one carefully out of the vase; it was like holding sapphires on a stem.

"I've never seen this color in a flower," I marveled.

Sandy cooed over the bouquet like it was a baby. The woman explained that they were blue gentians.

"Gentians?" I repeated.

"*Sí, señor.* They are gentians but very rare. They grow only in the Andes."

Sandy shook her head. "They are not just rare," she corrected the woman. "They barely exist. They are a mythical flower. It is said they give long life. I have never seen this many all at once. If you are lucky you may see one in your lifetime but to have a bouquet..."

I put my nose to the vase and sniffed carefully. For a second the odors of the market square disappeared. The smell of tobacco, of dust, of animals, of grilled meat and fresh wool and unfresh people, all vanished in an instant and was replaced by the cleanest, clearest air imaginable. The bouquet of asters had smelled sweet. The gentians smelled like life itself. I felt stronger from just one sniff.

But the color of the flowers was their most arresting feature. I had to have one, not only for myself but also for Walt because this flower, too, was on his list. Forget the vicuña, these gentians were incredible. I offered to buy the whole bouquet.

The lady smiled at my naiveté.

"No," she said politely. "*Nadie no vende estas flores.* You cannot buy gentians." Gently she retrieved the vase.

I explained that the flowers weren't for me, that there was someone who needed them for an important reason. The woman was unimpressed.

Sandy tried another tack. If we couldn't buy the flowers, she suggested, perhaps we could go pick some ourselves. She pleaded with the woman to tell where the gentians could be found. The woman refused to say. She pointed in a general way to the mountains behind the town. Her look told us that was all the information we would get.

"I can't give up that easily," I acknowledged as we turned away. "They are beautiful and just as important to me as the vicuña."

"Of course," Sandy replied. "Blue gentians are the vicuña of flowers! Except even more rare. Before the Inca even they were prized as the most beautiful flowers in the mountains. Their most sacred places were decorated with blue gentians. But that was when they grew everywhere. Now they are very hard to find."

"So is vicuña," I reminded her. "And we still haven't found that, either."

The woman with the flowers overheard my remark.

"You want vicuña?" she asked.

"Sí," I replied. "Do you know where I can find some?"

She eyed me carefully, studying my face as though suspecting there was more to the story but I had no desire to bring up Walt's dream again.

"No," she answered but then pointed between the stalls to our left. "But look over there."

Sandy and I hurried where she pointed. There were more tradesmen there but none of them knew anything about vicuña. I returned to the woman's table but found she had packed up and gone.

The sky turned cloudy and a few drops of rain fell. I circled the market twice more and was back in the same corner, still wondering which stall she had referred to, when I squeezed between two tents and found a familiar face on the verge of tears.

"Hola," I greeted her with a smile. "How are your hips?"

It was the girl from the dance class. Lisa. She stared at me, at first confused and then with relief.

"What?...Where?...How did you get here?" she stammered.

"My family brought me out."

"Your family...?" she repeated in disbelief. Then, remembering where she was, she looked at the shawl in her hands and at the man on the other side of the table. "Can you explain to him that I don't want this?" she pleaded, on the verge of tears. "I'm trying to find something smaller but can't make him understand. It's so frustrating. This day has been so bad..."

"Miguel's Translation at your service," I rushed to reply before she could start crying. "I can't order myself a decent lunch but two experts just taught me how to bargain for clothes."

I talked with the seller and explained what Lisa wanted. He threw up his hands and said of course, of course he could get her something closer to her size. He directed us to wait and dashed to a companion's table.

"You came just in time," Lisa said. She leaned against a pile of sweaters. "I'm about to have a nervous breakdown."

"Join the club. A while ago you could have seen me getting hysterical over flowers."

"No, I'm serious. This day has been a nightmare."

"Well," I said. "Maybe we can make it better. Let's get your shawl then I'll introduce you to my friends. We were just about to eat so you can tell us your ordeal there."

We found Karla and Sandy and the four of us sat down at a cafe. There Lisa told us about her day.

She had heard about Otavalo and planned to come on the public bus with a group from the language school. But on Friday the group backed out. Still wanting to make the trip she got up at four in the morning to go to the city terminal. Only then did she learn that Quito before sunup lacks much of the charm seen in tourist brochures. Vagrant dogs and homeless people wandered the streets. Street lights were out. Also, the terminal itself was in the least desirable area of the capital. Then she got on the wrong bus and was leaving the *south* side of town before she noticed. She hopped a cab back to the terminal but the cab driver took her somewhere else and demanded more money before he would take her where she wanted to go. By the time she got back to the terminal the only bus to Otavalo was full so she had to stand the entire trip. And it was a commuter, not a direct trip. She arrived long after the best bargaining times and only then realized that the Spanish she learned in one week at Simon Bolivar wasn't as good as she thought. She had trouble even buying a shawl. Thus the impending breakdown.

"*Ay, pobrecita!*" Sandy cried, taking Lisa's hand. "We will take you back to Quito. You can stay with us and we will make your day better."

That did make Lisa cry, this time in relief.

***

The afternoon was still young but soon we saw everything the market had to offer. And since the market *was* Otavalo, we had thus seen everything the town had to offer. When Sandy asked if we were ready to return to Quito I agreed.

"My only disappointment is the vicuña," I shrugged. "But I can tell my friend that I tried."

"What's vicuña?" Lisa asked.

I drew a picture in the dirt of the fragile animal and drew a huge alpaca next to it to show the contrast. Then I explained about the world's finest wool and why I wanted it.

"Nobody here raises the animals, sells the wool, or knows where to get it," I concluded. "That vendor by the fountain told me it's impossible and the flower lady was just confused."

Lisa cocked her head in thought and gazed off to the horizon where wispy clouds gathered over the caldera of Angochagua volcano.

"I know where you can find it," she announced.

We all stared at her. *"Dónde?"* Sandy demanded.

"On my way here this morning the bus turned off the highway. It went so long on a dirt road that when I realized it wasn't the way to Otavalo I got scared, thinking that no one would ever hear from me again. But the driver went to a village behind Angochagua. A bunch of people on the bus got off there. I don't know why but people were gathering in the square. There were signs and they all had the picture of that."

She pointed at my drawings in the dirt.

"The alpaca?"

"No, the small one. There were alpacas in the village but that's not what was on the signs."

I looked at Sandy and Karla. Sandy translated for her friend and Karla became excited.

"Qué hacía la gente en el pueblo?"

Lisa shrugged.

"I don't know what they were doing. People were dressed up. When they got off the bus they couldn't have gone far. It's open countryside up there and the village isn't big."

We hurried to the car.

Lisa was right that Angochagua wasn't big but the mountains behind it were. Sandy's Corolla chugged eight miles up the dirt road and if we were ever on less than a four-percent grade it was only long enough to build up speed for the next climb. When we reached the village the elevation surpassed ten thousand feet.

"We can't stay long," Sandy advised. "We must be back on the road to Quito before it gets dark."

That proved easier said than done. The crowd from Lisa's bus was nowhere to be found and the first person we asked explained where they had gone.

"It's a *chaccu*," an old man in a floppy hat explained. *"Allá."* He pointed east. There our road curved through the settlement and exited onto the *páramo* beyond. Miles away we could see people walking, getting ever smaller in the distance.

"What's a chaccu?" I asked.

The man explained it was an annual event in villages throughout the Andes where indigenous people used traditional methods to gather livestock.

"A roundup?"

"Qué es un roundup?"

I explained the American version.

"Sí," he shrugged. "Then it's a roundup!" He was pleased to know the English word.

"And it's a roundup of vicuña?" Karla clarified.

The man nodded. The chaccu would take place miles away out on the páramo, the high plains of the Andes. And it wasn't until tomorrow.

"I cannot stay until tomorrow," Sandy apologized after the old man walked away.

"Ay, pobrecito!" lamented Karla. "Neither can I. We must return tonight."

Shadows crept across the valley as the sun sank toward the horizon. I knew she was right. We would have to go soon – the thought of driving the Pan American highway in the dark made my muscles tense. But still…a vicuña was near. We would never get back in time tomorrow to catch the event.

Reluctantly we started to load back into the car. Then Sandy stopped.

"*Pues*," she announced. "Miguel, *you* should stay."

"*Cómo?*" Karla demanded.

"*Sí*, he should stay. *Este es el Ecuador*. It is our country. We have much to show him, remember? Who else has a chaccu? When will he ever see one again?"

"But he cannot stay. Where will he stay? He is out here all alone."

"He will be fine," Sandy insisted. "The villagers will take care of him."

In truth I wanted to stay but worried that abandoning them would be rude.

"But you cannot stay here by yourself," Karla argued.

"I've been in worse places," I reassured her. "I'll find a way back to Quito."

"I'll come with you!" Lisa announced. We all stared at her, whereupon she added, "if that's okay."

Karla and Sandy looked at her like she had two heads. Lisa should have had enough of Ecuadorian back roads by now.

"You'll miss your classes," I reminded her. "It might take a few days to get back."

"I'm here on a grant," she shrugged. "Besides, I'll practice Spanish just as much out here."

"*Bueno! Eso es!*" Sandy announced, pleased with herself. She clapped her hands. Karla wasn't so sure. It was with obvious misgivings that she got back in the car and allowed her friend to point them down the mountain. I knew she felt protective of me as her house guest. There was also jealousy in the air as the two of them drove away and she waved good-bye. Lisa had interloped and stolen her American.

"Will she be mad at you now?" Lisa asked, guessing my thoughts as the sound of the Corolla died away.

I watched the car disappear in a cloud of dust down the hill.

"Maybe. But not if I find something to like about Ecuador."

***

There were enough people left in Angochagua that we found a place to spend the night. It was a restaurant but the owners were happy to accept five dollars apiece from Lisa and me for two rooms in the back.

In the morning, following instructions from the cook we awoke before dawn and followed a thin line of people straggling east out of town. The air was dry and frigid. I was grateful the *otavaleño* had talked me into buying his poncho the day before. Lisa walked beside me wrapped in a shawl.

"Where are we going?" she whispered. The trail descended gently to a vast plain. It stretched for miles and grew wider the farther we walked. In the distance Cotopaxi volcano and its twin Cayumbe loomed against a lightening sky. We trod a hillside trail surrounded by green and yellow grasses of the *páramo*. Meadows of the same color stretched into the distance.

"I don't know."

By noon we had walked ten miles. The sky cleared and despite the altitude the air warmed. The land rolled up to the base of the volcanoes and flowed around them, turning broad and green and flattening into pastures. Eucalyptus forests ringed the summits. The line of people grew longer as stragglers joined from both sides. We grew tired but the otherworldly landscape convinced us not to ask anyone how far we were going.

Finally the goal of our efforts came in sight: on a swathe of land wide enough to hold Quito itself a tent appeared, then a series of corrals, and then people converging on both from all directions.

"What is it?" I asked aloud.

A woman near me replied, *"Es el chaccu."*

The chaccu had a carnival atmosphere. We approached the tents and found no vehicles. No music, either, except for a handful of men with pipes. If anyone brought food it wasn't in sight. Yet people mingled with enthusiasm and scanned the hillsides for new arrivals. The air warmed and more tents went up to ward off the sun. Lisa and I found space under a lean-to whose other inhabitants happily made room, surprised but delighted to see us in their ranks. The mood was holiday-friendly. Eventually there were a thousand individuals clustered on the plain and an air of anticipation ran through us all, even those of us who didn't know what we were waiting for.

"We're the only non-natives here," Lisa whispered.

"Yes."

"Do you think someone will mind?"

I looked around the lean-to and at the people milling outside. No one paid us any attention. The few times when someone did look our way the look was always accompanied by a smile.

"Not so far."

After an hour a murmur went up at the south side of the gathering. People stood up to look that way. Lisa and I left the lean-to.

"Is someone coming?"

On the horizon hung a cloud of dust, low and flat like a seam between the ground and sky. At first I thought it was riders but the cloud wasn't high or deep the way it would be if something heavy like horses or vehicles kicked it up. There was no distant rumble of hooves to announce the coming of a herd, the way there would have been with cattle.

Another murmur ran through the crowd. People drew off in two directions, each on an angle to the coming cloud. The tent area emptied. Rather than be left behind Lisa and I fell in with the group spreading to the west side.

"What are we doing?" Lisa asked but it was clear from her tone that she didn't need to know. The mood of the crowd was electric; it was easy to feel part of the event even if the details were unclear. Besides, once out from under the lean-to we were overwhelmed by the immensity of the Andean highlands. The valley we were in was so wide we felt microscopic on its floor.

Another feature that lent size to our surroundings was underfoot. The ground was hard but grass grew everywhere, waist-high like winter wheat. It was of all types and colors and the tallest plants were split at their stalks and going to seed so that feathery tendrils rode the breeze and spread ripples across the valley floor. Shale lay everywhere. The pieces were sharp but grass rose between them and waved with a softness that belied the soil. Wildflowers grew in uncountable numbers.

Lisa laughed as the wind blew her hair and moved swells through the acres of tall grass.

"I know what we're doing!" she cried. "We're art. Living art."

The cloud of dust approached.

"No," I told her, finally figuring it out. "We're a fence."

The base of the cloud changed color. It became tan and then auburn and then a rusty red that shimmered in the heat. The cloud itself remained thin, spread wide on the plain. Gradually it acquired droplets, outriders, individual figures on the edges that weaved beside the main body.

There was still no rumble but as the herd came on a gentle hiss preceded it.

Our line shifted. The people far to our right backed up as did the people facing them in the opposite line a thousand yards away. They spread wide but the locals nearby urged us to hold our position.

I kept my spacing from Lisa and pointed into the oncoming mass.

"We're a fence. Actually, now we're a funnel. They'll come right by here and get squeezed smaller and smaller until they have no choice but to go into the corrals."

"Who's they?" Lisa demanded, peering into the dust cloud. "Who'll come right by?" Then suddenly individual animals became distinct and answered her question. As her eyes widened at the sight the lady to her left confirmed it.

"*La vicuña,*" she said, beaming. "They've come."

Where the animals came from I have no idea. Why they agreed to come I don't know, either. And how the men herding them were able to keep up, jogging alongside with cheers and whistles and managing to breathe and see through the dust that coated them in páramo yellow until they were the same color as the ground they trod was most incomprehensible of all. But the herd came.

The vicuña appeared. Immediately after them came the men. We heard their whoops and calls, their voices rejoicing in work and none of their enthusiasm lost on the wind. Underneath the calls was the hiss, a tympanic tinkle of thousands of hooves knocking on shale that sounded like rain hitting a city street. But it should have been no surprise to me how this herd danced across the earth. These animals weren't livestock, after all. They were free spirits combed gently from mountain slopes in a relationship that had survived thousands of years in a land where hardier domestics were unknown, docile creatures who relished the crisp air of open countryside but who had learned to accept the kleptocratic habits of their warmth-challenged neighbors. The vicuña trotted past with heads held high and no fear on their doe-like faces. They were the aristocracy of the llamanid genus and seemed to know it. As proof, the men following them held no tools of persuasion beyond their vocal cords. There were no bolos of the gaucho or lariats of the cowboy or bullwhips of the vaquero in this crowd. In the hands of these *chagras* there was nothing but respect.

"Vaya! Vaya! Cerca!" came calls from the right. Our lines collapsed as the vicuña rushed by. The farthest people curled around to join up behind the *chagras* and press the herd forward. The rest of us faced toward the corrals and slid parallel to the drove.

"They're beautiful!" Lisa cried.

There were hundreds of animals, some as tall as Lisa. They cantered between our ranks in close order. The adults eyed us with haughty curiosity rather than fear, turning their slender necks in a manner that suggested they found amusing our concept of a fence. Younger animals trotted alongside the adults. All had shaggy coats. The body and necks were brown while white reached across the bellies and up around the mouths like a muzzle. En masse the herd looked like nothing so much as a convocation of exclusive but unkempt white-tailed deer.

"They're tiny," I commented.

"They're not tiny, they're as tall as you," Lisa corrected me.

"Yes, but look at their frames. They're light, fragile."

Perhaps hearing my slight a handful of vicuña bulged toward our line at that moment. They were only jostling for position but the sudden movement made Lisa and me step back. The lady next to Lisa laughed. She held an infant and led a two-year-old boy by the hand and jabbered something that we gathered said we had nothing to fear. But when the line bulged a second time and this time the vicuña surged toward her she barked a startled command at the boy. He stumbled and fell, leaving her hand. The nearest vicuna would have stepped on him had Lisa not reached in and snatched him out of harm's way at the last moment. The animal bounced against her but she held on. The herd moved on. Once clear Lisa put him on her shoulders, from which perch he glared eye-level at the creatures who had almost trod him under.

***

Shearing the animals took the rest of the afternoon. The locals had a large crowd but were still outnumbered by the herd. Soon half of our gathering was inside the fences and mingling with the animals. The other half, mostly women, sat in rows under the tents sorting through great bags of wool delivered from the corral. Lisa's boy, once the herd was in the corral, returned to his mother but soon grew bored. After a while he made a dash for the corral, being small enough that he could have easily slipped under the lowest fence rail where the vicuna mingled and their thin, strong legs kicked and stomped in the earth. The mother cried out and once again Lisa grabbed the boy before he could be trampled. This time she handed him to me.

"You're now a baby-sitter," she informed me. The boy scrabbled for my shoulders so I swung him into place there. He laughed at his new vantage point. The crowd of women clapped their approval.

"The hell I am. She can have her kid back..."

"And what then?" Lisa stopped me as I moved to put the boy back on his feet. "Do you know how to shear a vicuña?"

"Um, no."

"Neither do I. Nor do I know how to clean wool, or spin it, or weave it, or anything else. So you might want to hang onto the one job you can do."

***

Vicuña

The sea will always have its way. The sky, too, with seamless depths of ancient blue and black of endless days and nights that pour across the landscape and claim it for their own. Prairies in the spring and forest floors of russet leaves claim "Here I am and I am all that is," for a time. But time and constancy are not all. The world is small. The world is vast. What we create will never last and yet...There is beauty in the impermanent – in the loving touch of wind, in the meeting of two minds, and in the gathering of rituals that once gathered will never be the same. There is beauty in the fleeting glimpse of tender creatures white in soul and conscience as in face. There is beauty in their freedom, in the wind-swept liberty of frozen nights on the shingles of the world and in the warm honor with which they trade it, time on time, for the pious cold company of us. There is beauty in the impermanent, and I have seen that beauty.

"Tu eres poeta?" Sandy asked, astonished, looking up from the piece of paper.

"Sí," Lisa told her.

"You said you were a writer," I reminded her.

"I am. I write poetry."

I leaned over Sandy's shoulder and read the words myself, looking for an explanation. Not that I expected to find any. Prose such as Lisa's didn't do anything for me. Reading the musings of somebody on a bowl of apples or a summer afternoon or a chaccu wasn't my idea of entertainment. But neither was lecturing Lisa on her profession. What was on my mind as I sought enlightenment from her page was how bothered I should be by Walt's dream.

"For a living?"

"Not a good living but yes. Why, does that bother you? You look upset."

I put her poem down and took up the pullover hanging on Sandy's chair. After the *chaccu* the boy's mother had given it to Lisa for saving her child. It was twice Lisa's size so she in turn had passed it to me. Light, almost weightless, with threads so fine they could have been silk, the wool was warm to the touch.

"No, it's just that... life gets more interesting every day."

Oh, hell. I had the vicuña, I was still in one piece, and I was sitting around a kitchen table with three cute girls. One of them just happened to write poetry. But how did Walt know?

"You've never met a poet?" Lisa asked.

I said no and passed the sweater to Karla, who held it out to admire. "But now I know one," she smiled.

Lisa reached in her backpack and pulled out a thin volume with a yellow cover and torn edges. She handed it to Karla who flipped through the pages. She didn't read English but seeing Lisa's name on the cover was sufficient to impress her.

"Léalo a mí," she said, handing it to me. "Read it to me."

I took it but Lisa closed it on me and put it back in her bag.

"I'm still shy about people actually reading my stuff," she explained. "Especially strangers."

"But you wrote that poem. Will you put that in a book, too?"

"Maybe. Maybe I'll write a whole book of poems just on this trip." She sighed and stared up at the ceiling. "I had never imagined anything like that chaccu," she said. "Or those mountains. That valley was the most beautiful place anyone could think of. Those meadows, those people."

"Magical," I agreed. "I've never seen anything like it."

"Do you mean that?" Karla asked.

"Of course."

She swelled with pride and smiled like I hadn't seen her do since I fell onto her floor.

2

EVAN

One of my first missions as pilot in command was to fly some people to a small airfield in the Andes mountains. It didn't go well. We got the passengers there in one piece but the weather was bad, I got us stuck in clouds longer than planned, and ice formed all over the aircraft. For a while we had to descend into the mountains and pick our way through unknown valleys. It gave the whole crew a scare, and a good pilot should never scare his crew.

To make sure the experience hadn't scared *me* away from mountains, our commander ordered Walt to get me back down around the Andes as much as possible.

Evan was also on Walt's fly list. Evan had gone to language school and then done a short tour as "Sam," our ground-pounding liaison officer to the Army, up at Soto Cano Air Base in Honduras. So he had been out of the cockpit for months. Walt wanted him to get current again but also hoped to tap Evan's oddness for the treasure hunt. For difficult items like the sisal and the stele, Walt reckoned he needed more unique personalities on the job.

That was how one day Evan and I were tasked to fly to the town of Lucmayo in central Peru. Lucmayo was one of a trio of villages high in the Ayacucho district that relied on the Plateado Reservoir for water, using it to feed a thousand people along with their livestock and crops. The Plateado was an inland lake at 8,600 feet up in the mountains. It had been there since time immemorial but one night after an earthquake it began to drain. Within forty-eight hours it was gone, leaving villagers in shock at the edges of a dry bowl a mile square and a hundred feet deep. It also left us tasked to provide them humanitarian assistance.

Lucmayo was a disaster but it was a strange one. Normally mountain villages suffered from avalanches or floods, not a sudden drought. The first supplies we carried in reflected the confusion: left-over desalination kits from Pisco, a coastal town which the year before had been hit by a tsunami.

"You want us to carry desalination kits to a mountain village?" I queried the aid worker in Pisco. "They don't have salt water in the mountains. They don't have any water – that's the problem."

"I don't care what they have or don't have," the Red Cross worker replied. "We had a disaster here on the coast a year ago and people from around the world sent us so much aid that we have stuff left over. We have to make sure it gets used or no one will send us aid in the future."

"But a tsunami on the coast is a different disaster than a drought in the mountains," I persisted. "Don't you have jugs of water we can take instead?"

"No. Take the desalination kits or go home."

We were naive enough to accept the kits and the reasoning that produced them, thinking the aid community knew what it was doing and that there was a bigger picture we didn't see. But once airborne we appreciated just how awkward our cargo was.

"We should dump this stuff," I suggested as we flew down the coast. "Just dump it in the ocean, then go back to Pisco and say we delivered the kits and are ready for real aid."

"No," Evan replied. "They'll just give us something else the villagers don't need, like a ton of saltine crackers or a pallet of dehydrated peaches."

So we didn't dump the kits. We kept them on board and flew as far as Nazca before turning to cross the mountains.

Overflying Nazca meant overflying the Nazca Lines. I knew about the Nazca Lines because Evan knew about them. Evan knew about them because in college the geology department cancelled his tuition assistance in order to buy the football team new uniforms. To pay for his classes he worked nights at a peanut-processing plant near Marietta, Georgia, where five nights a week he climbed into giant vats with a hydrometer to measure the moisture content of the nuts. Then at three in the morning he drove home, cruising through the middle of the night when there was nothing on the radio worth listening to except the AM talk shows. The best of those was Coast-to-Coast, the essential conspiracy-theorist program on which Art Bell discussed everything from how the Rothschild family owned the Federal Reserve to why black helicopters were responsible for cattle mutilations near Cheyenne. Driving through the night, Evan learned there were underground alien cities in New Mexico, that the 1986 airstrikes on Libya had really been carried out to recover the Ark of the Covenant, and how 'grays' or 'shadow people' skewed results of the 1980 census. He also learned about the Nazca Lines.

Nazca is a dusty town eighty miles south of Pisco. It sits in the desert and is unremarkable except for huge geometric shapes carved into the ground on a plateau outside the city. The shapes are of all kinds: a monkey, a lizard, a spider, and various triangles and circles. Archeologists estimate the designs to be at least two thousand years old. Since they're on a flat expanse of desert and most are hundreds of feet long, it's impossible to see them from the ground. The only way to see even one complete design is to view it from an elevation of several hundred feet. But you can't do that outside of a plane. There are no mountains, hills, or buttes around to give one that perspective. So why did the Nazca Indians, a culture that died out around 800 A.D., draw figures in the sand that they could never see for themselves?

Some scientists guessed the lines were used to track the seasons. Others believed they were part of religious rituals. Evan knew the truth: alien spaceships.

In fact, Evan figured the Nazca were aliens. The drawings were landing zones. Their culture didn't die out as archeologists believed: instead the people simply left, taking their spaceships back to where they had come from.

His explanations found doubters in our squadron. Really? Lowell would ask. How interesting. But why did the aliens come to the middle of nowhere in Peru in the first place? Why not Rome, for example, or Cairo, or any other populous city of the time?

The aliens had already been to Cairo, Evan would reply. Who did Lowell think built the pyramids? Egyptians, Lowell would answer, convinced that Evan had inhaled too many peanut fumes. Evan would smile at our naiveté. Egyptians, he scoffed. Sure.

Alien-made or not, from three miles up we could see the lines clearly. They were cave pictograms, pure and simple; stamped out on the ground by people moving rocks instead of scraped on walls with charcoal but with the same graphic innocence of a child looking at a pet and drawing what he sees. After listening to Evan's musings, I had trouble seeing them as just pictures but still didn't see landing zones. You definitely had to be an alien – or on drugs – to look at the drawings and see any direction to final approach.

But Evan saw it.

"That way," he said as we passed overhead.

"Beg your pardon?"

"We should go that way."

"Why? Lucmayo is off the nose."

"Yeah," he agreed, peering out his side window to study the drawings. "But we know going to Lucmayo is pointless. Down there it says there's a field four degrees right of course. Still in the Barroso region but not Lucmayo. So let's go that way. Maybe we'll find someone who needs desalination kits."

I looked out my window to see where he was getting all his information.

"Evan, that's a lizard. It's not directions to an airport."

"You have to look at the whole mural of pictures," he explained, undaunted. "That is a lizard, true, but you don't navigate a low-level by looking at only one leg of the route, do you?"

"I don't navigate anywhere by looking at lizards."

"Okay, but just in case Lucmayo doesn't work out..."

"I'll keep it in mind."

Lucmayo didn't work out. It was heartbreaking to see the hope on the villagers' faces when we arrived and painful to see their emotions turn to anger when they broke open the first boxes and saw our cruel gift. We explained the Pisco situation but they threw up their hands and stalked off. So we took off just as full as we landed and headed back to the coast.

"Want to try where the lizard was pointing?" Evan yawned forty miles later.

"The lizard wasn't pointing anywhere," I insisted.

"Sure," he replied but then began to pout so I checked our gas and did some quick math. "Okay, Space Man, I'll give you twenty minutes."

He yanked a map from his pocket and spun a solution on his whiz wheel. "Over there," he pointed. "To the right of that peak. Maybe ten miles."

I followed his directions. The terrain was dry but in the distance we saw the tip of a glacier and snow on the peaks. Evan was lecturing me on the similarities between the Nazca lines and Masonic architecture when we suddenly passed by a giant snake carved into the side of a bluff. He whooped in delight.

"Gettin' close!"

In a few minutes we were overhead a small and very old town nestled in the crook of a mountain pass. It was a thousand feet lower than Lucmayo but in the same chain of hills. On the side of the mountain there was a road leading to the town that disappeared a mile short, smothered in a shiny rock slide that cascaded down an escarpment to the bottom of the pass and a moraine below. Beside the slide was a pond.

Beyond the town and far from the pond a stream felt its way out of the pass. It coursed in stair-stepping drops off the plateau. As it fell the water passed an old rail line built on an impossible grade.

Where the rails topped out and entered the town there was a flat area wide enough for a couple of parade grounds. After circling twice and attracting attention we landed. I turned the plane around within a hundred yards of the water.

The mayor met us.

We had interrupted a gathering at the water's edge. People lined the shore of the two-acre pool or scrambled around the rocks beside it. The middle of the pond bubbled as though from an underground jet. The disturbance rocked the surface and caused water to overflow the rocks, explaining why they glistened from above.

"Who are you?" the mayor asked. "We didn't expect anyone for days."

We explained the relief effort at Lucmayo. I wanted Evan to expound on his lizard theory but when his Spanish proved unequal to the task I made up a story about how the people at Lucmayo had urged us to explore down the mountain for other victims of the earthquake. The mayor nodded in enthusiasm at the lie.

"*Buen' cosa* that they did," he enthused. "You can tell the government that Otoca is cut off. You see our road – it is gone! This...this..." he waved his hand behind him at the rock slide, "this took our road."

The rock slide looked even bigger up close. The left wall of the pass had given way and slid to the plateau's edge. Huge chunks of limestone and slate were now strewn across a half-dozen acres. Bits of the slate had drawings on them, something Evan picked up on immediately. Stick figures of animals, wide eyeballs, the sun and stars and who knows what else lay scattered across and in the pond, less ambitious rock drawings to accompany the snake we had just passed. Evan was overjoyed.

"That just happened?" I asked.

"Yesterday morning," the mayor nodded.

"But the earthquake was last week."

"We never felt the earthquake."

"It was huge. How could you not feel it?"

He shrugged. The man had a lively glance and eyebrows that grew together.

"We never felt the earthquake," he repeated flatly. "We heard about it from people coming up the mountain but it didn't move anything here. Then yesterday, out of nowhere..." he waved his hand again and turned to face the water.

"The rock slide?" Evan prompted.

"No! *El agua.*"

Evan and I looked at each other.

"The water overflowed its banks?" I guessed. "After the earthquake?"

"There was no earthquake!" the mayor barked. "And there are no banks!"

"But the water…"

"There was no water! Until yesterday morning our only water was there." He pointed beyond our aircraft to the small stream.

Evan and I looked at each other, confused.

"That stream is enough for this town?" I asked.

"No," the mayor sighed. "It flows less and less which is why our town is dying. A thousand years people have lived here – a thousand years! – but now the water cannot keep up. We have to send people down the mountain to bring it in. That is why this is bad. Our road was open – then this…"

He pointed back to the water. It took a moment for what he was saying to sink in.

"This pool just appeared?" Evan asked.

"*Sí.*"

"What? How?"

"Are you not listening? It just *appeared*. There was no earthquake here. Until yesterday morning everything was fine – then *boosh!* Water burst up and pushed the whole hillside down."

We walked to the water's edge. People gathered around as though expecting an explanation. If so they were disappointed. I stood at the water's edge and stared at it like everyone else, watching the turbulence in the center of the pond and the ripples that spread out to lap at my feet.

On closer inspection it was obvious the pool was new: as the mayor said, there were no banks. There was just a wide deep hole. It looked like a water main had broken and bubbled up to the surface, blasting a reservoir in the process.

"What was here?" it occurred to me to ask. "Not houses, I hope."

"No, no houses," the mayor crossed himself. "A mine." He gestured toward the water with one hand and the old rail line behind us with the other as though that would explain everything.

"Coal? Gold?"

He laughed bitterly. "We do not have that kind of luck. Anyway, it was emptied out years ago."

"Well," I said, trying to cheer him up. "At least you have water again."

He shook his head. "As I said, we do not have that kind of luck."

I didn't understand what he meant but Evan knelt down and swirled the water. Then he licked his fingers. His eyes lit up in comprehension.

"Una mina de sal," he told the mayor. "You had a salt mine."

"Si," the man agreed. "It was never much. They stopped digging years ago. It was too shallow – but it was deep enough."

"What do you mean?" I asked him.

"It means it was deep enough that this is where the water decided to bubble up," Evan explained. "It also means they can't drink the water."

A man next to the mayor heard him and exclaimed *Si!* in an angry voice. He reached down and cupped a handful of water to bring to his lips. Immediately he spat it out, the action eliciting a bitter look from everyone around.

"Salt water," Evan repeated with a chuckle. "They can't drink it because it's salty."

"I'm glad you think our situation is funny," the mayor accused him. "We are the victims of God's joke, not you!"

Evan's smile grew wider. "You're not victims!" he shot back, motioning for me to translate. "You just won the lottery!" When my translation produced confusion – including my own – Evan cupped some of the water himself. "This is calcium chloride," he explained, letting the water run through his fingers and then rubbing the grit that remained. "It's a nothing deposit – look, you can see the break in the wall. With a flow like this the salt will wash out of here in a matter of weeks. That's why the miners stopped digging." To my skeptical look he added, "Hey, I didn't spend all four years in a peanut vat. My degree is in rocks."

The mayor and his crowd grew animated. Nobody was ready to take Evan at his word but since they were still in shock they were willing to grasp at the lifeline he offered.

"And it gets better," Evan added.

"How could it get better?" I asked, anxious to hear what shoe he would drop next.

"Have you forgotten what we're carrying?"

Of course. Evan danced a jig in self-satisfaction as I explained to the mayor about the desalination kits. They weren't much – and maybe the villagers would suck the stream dry before they agreed to strain the flat, tasteless kit water through their teeth – but it was a fix if they needed it. With hugs all around the people on the plateau celebrated our crew as saviors.

***

"You're a hero," I told my copilot later as we watched a handful of villagers carry the last boxes off the plane.

"Yep," he yawned.

"The mayor wants to give us a reward. You can probably have your pick of the local women. Too bad Jem's not here."

"Nah, I already told him what we want."

"You did? What?"

"Oh, come on. I've got to suck up to the man back home. Walt's getting me all these flying hours so I have to say thanks." He went to the ramp where our loadmaster Paul had a cargo strap wrapped around a thick object covered with a blanket. Two men from the village were slinging it carefully forward in the cabin. When they set it down, Evan pulled the blanket free to reveal a slab of the basalt from the water's edge. The rock was still wet but its face was otherwise drab, a lusterless black scored with deep lines to show a primitive and ancient shooting star.

"A petroglyph, of course," I nodded, vexed with myself for forgetting the list.

"Yep. There are a bunch over there but I thought this one was appropriate." Evan ran his hands gently over the rock, tracing the furrows that some artist from a millennium earlier had seen fit to carve. "Showing the space ship and all – I thought that would appeal to Walt's little quest."

"That's a shooting star, Evan," I corrected him. "A shooting star, not a space ship."

He chuckled, his fingers never leaving the stone. Evan wasn't an expressive guy – in the months that I had known him, asleep and awake were the only emotional extremes he seemed to have. But now he was positively content.

"A shooting star," he smiled. "Sure."

3

SPIES, FLIES, AND SHRUNKEN HEADS

We didn't get intelligence briefs for most of our operations. Sometimes the Wing would send someone to our hangar to give an overview of events in a particular country but for the most part when we flew someplace it was with just enough knowledge to get our job done.

For that reason nobody minded when Little Bud volunteered for a short course in intelligence up in the States. His was a jumpy and abrasive personality but we figured if he learned something that could help us do our jobs safer then more power to him.

He didn't. We're not sure what he studied in Texas. He came back just as intense and paranoid as before and with no perceivable difference in what he had to offer regarding his knowledge of rebels, drug runners, or dictatorial governments. The only twist was that now he was prone to level glares and solemn pronouncements about how we "didn't know what we didn't know." He had become a spy.

He thought he was a spy, anyway. Worse, he was a spy and we were all traitors. From the moment he returned from intelligence training, Little Bud did everything short of don a trench coat and fedora to eavesdrop on his fellow aircrew. Have a conversation at the ops desk – Little Bud was there. Whine about the flying schedule over lunch

– Little Bud was there. Take off late from Bogotá because the whole crew was hung over after a night in the Zona Rosa – Little Bud may or may not be there but somehow he heard about it. He became a master of eavesdropping.

"You never know what's important," was his response in the club one day when Josh demanded to know why he couldn't mind his own business. "History turns on the strangest things."

"This isn't history," Josh would point out. "It's my lunch. Go away before I beat you."

But Little Bud wouldn't go away. The more people chased him off, the more he became convinced that the entire squadron was a threat to national security.

That was fine as far as it went and for a while we indulged his suspicions by staging mock conversations when he was around. "You get the stuff?" Lowell would ask me in a whisper from his cubicle, knowing that Little Bud was only two desks down and listening. "Not here," I would whisper back, whereupon Lowell would get impatient and insist that "his people" needed product by the end of the week or he would be in deep trouble. Jake went further by learning a few phrases in Russian that he would whisper over the phone to a dial tone whenever Bud entered the room, and Charlie Manson once wrapped a blanket around a Life Support dummy and made sure Little Bud saw him stuffing it into the trunk of his car.

But we realized we had overreached when the commander's exec, Mystic Pete, informed us that Little Bud was doing more than just listening in. He was writing everything down and delivering voluminous weekly reports to the squadron leadership.

The reports covered what everyone in the squadron was doing. It transcribed them with equal amounts of fervor, from invented hoaxes like Jake's Russian to real events like Evan's dalliances with Chorillo hookers and my totaling a Mercedes on D Street while drunk off my ass. Little Bud even described in detail Walt's treasure hunt and noted who was picking up what and where they were landing to get it. That alone should have gotten most of us court-martialed.

But fortunately the reports went nowhere. Little Bud was afraid of Lt Col Rasmussen and didn't pass him his notes directly. Instead he went to the Assistant Director of Ops, or ADO. Every Friday he stomped into Maj Byron's office and threw down his Harriet the Spy diary of the squadron's disreputable activities, demanding that the Air Force take action. And every Friday Byron ignored the folder and instead made Little Bud sit through four or five gunship videos from the Panama invasion. When Byron transferred out, Little Bud moved up the chain of command to Major Farnham and pled his case there. Farnham paid even less attention to his tales. He nodded and smiled, half-listening to Little Bud's description of a viper's nest of treacherous behavior in the 155th while thinking instead of whatever Farnham thought about at moments like that, then he would encourage Bud to keep up the good work, shoo him out of the room, and drop the report into a drawer without reading it. When Farnham left for the day, Mystic Pete would take the file and shred it. Then the seven-day cycle would repeat itself.

So in that respect Little Bud's spying was a bust. Nobody ever took his surveillance activities seriously and nobody was ever hurt by his documentation of our transgressions. In fact, contrary to his intentions someone actually benefited from his overblown patriotism, for it was only through his mole-ish behavior that Walt found his skull.

***

By "his" I don't mean that Walt found his own skull, or that he found Little Bud's. I mean he finally found the one he had seen in his dream, the one held up on a long arm thrust out of the earth somewhere on the South American continent.

That was an accomplishment for in spite of obvious reasons to believe that such an object would be elusive Walt instead convinced himself early on that acquiring it would be simple. And sure enough, not long into the hunt he found a skull in Puyo, Ecuador, that he thought would satisfy his nocturnal vision.

The Puyo skull – found in a bookstore – had laughing eyes and a firm jaw. The only problem was that it was fake. It was a plaster scientific model, not a real head. Walt acknowledged that but in the enthusiasm of discovery he determined at first that a plaster skull was good enough. It looked real, it was in Ecuador, and he had had to go to an out-of-the-way place to find it. Should he look a gift skull in the mouth?

But no sooner was the skull brought to Panama and placed in his collection than he began to have second thoughts. Some inner voice told him that a plaster model wouldn't do. As the rest of us assembled bona fide items – objects like the Korubo war club and a Copan sisal that guys took real risks to obtain – the molded grin on the shelf became less triumphant and more mocking. Doubt crept in. Walt got to where he couldn't look at the thing.

Finally his conscience won over: he threw the plaster skull in the trash and told the rest of us to keep searching. But where he expected us to search no one knew. Rolo suggested half-seriously that we just rob a graveyard.

As if reading Rolo's mind, Kurt and Skinny Steve later made a four-wheel-drive excursion to the Darien region of Panama in a futile attempt to travel overland to Colombia for vacation. En route they accidentally drove through a cemetery where their monster tires unearthed a skeleton from a shallow grave. Being who they were, they thought nothing of keeping it. There was no doubt about *that* skull being genuine.

Walt was repulsed when they brought it to them, as were the rest of us. But unlike the rest of us he had a mission to fulfill so he looked past his revulsion, washed the thing off, and stuck it on the shelf to give it a chance. He figured if he could still stand to look at it after a few weeks then it passed the guilt test and would stay in the collection.

But he couldn't and it didn't. Walt was soon tormented by new dreams. These were of bleached craniums leaping from the shelf and running away on tiny feet, or flying away on downy wings, or driving away in tiny cars – however they did it, they were leaving. When the dreams continued Walt interpreted them to mean that once again he had the wrong skull. That interpretation was buttressed by the fact that one day the skull went missing and the dreams stopped. Kurt later admitted that he stole the skull back in order to impress an enlisted girl he was dating, but then she made him feel so guilty over how he obtained it that he returned the whole skeleton to the Darien and chucked it back into the weeds.

***

Enter Declan.

Declan was somebody who actually got along with Little Bud. One reason was that Declan was so pleasantly self-absorbed that he didn't pay attention when Bud did things that the rest of us found maddening. Declan was able to see what drives people and he correctly saw that Little Bud, though a jerk, wasn't trying to be one. He just liked attention.

Another reason Declan grew close to Little Bud was because of the latter's tattle-tale journals. As clever and imaginative and well-spoken as Declan was, he was nevertheless a kept man. He was married and led a boring life away from most of the squadron. So he lived vicariously through the rest of us. He was always begging people to come by the house and tell him what they were doing. He started home-brewing beer just to entice people in the door. He became a master at ferreting out who had what agenda in the squadron and who was opposed, and then talking both groups into coming over to his house to work it out just so he could have the company. So when he heard about Little Bud's surreptitious record-keeping, he did everything he could to get Bud to visit.

That proved difficult. Little Bud wasn't tracking our doings because he wanted to be a Hollywood reporter – he was trying to save the nation. He wasn't going to reveal what he discovered simply because Declan was a bored voyeur. So Declan had to ply him with more than just beer to get him to open up. He had to bait Little Bud with stories of his own. "Did you hear what Lowell's up to with the general's daughter?" he would whisper to Little Bud at the hangar. "Come by after dinner and I'll fill you in."

The only hitch to Declan's scheme was that he had no stories. If he did, he wouldn't have needed Little Bud. No problem – he made them up.

Thus for months Little Bud would stop by Declan's every Sunday night to get liquored up on homebrew and engage in a gossip fest. There he would learn how Flutie had dated a mother and daughter for weeks and gone to great lengths to keep either of them from finding out about the other; how the Cali Cartel was after Major Byron because he had agreed to smuggle a pallet of cocaine but then got cold feet and dumped it in the ocean; how half the lieutenants in the squadron were owners of a child slavery ring in Iquitos; and how the C-27 mechanics had a deal with Chinese traders in Colón to swap our American-made engines for cheaper imported parts.

The ruse worked for a while. Declan fed Little Bud ever wilder and more salacious tales and in return found out – to his glee – which 19-year-old airman Kurt had recently bagged and how much money Josh had won or lost in the Lima casinos. Little Bud ate it up, happily showing what he knew and thinking he had found an inside man.

But eventually Declan's stories unraveled. First, they conflicted with information Little Bud found out on his own. While it was true, for example, that a few of the loadmasters had organized the kids in Iquitos, it was for purposes of tracking and procuring women, not child slavery. And while there were – as Declan pointed out and Little Bud already knew – many unauthorized landings going on among crews downrange, it was not – as Declan claimed – part of an under-the-table agreement with evangelical groups whereby some of us filled our own collection plates ferrying missionaries around. Little Bud knew we were doing it to pick up Walt's junk. He still thought that was treason but it had nothing to do with Lutherans.

Declan's claims were also inconsistent. He loved any stories that had to do with lesbianism and would frequently claim that this spouse or that girlfriend was a practitioner. He linked Billie the lawyer with Mark Jonkris' girlfriend, for example, an image that even I couldn't object to. But then he would talk about some officer dallying with prostitutes (another favorite theme) and lament the man's "long-suffering wife" – a wife he had earlier described as a Sapphic nymphomaniac – leaving even the gullible Little Bud to say "huh?"

So Little Bud began to suspect that Declan was a fraud and soon Declan was back on his own, feeling left out and bored. Abandoned by Little Bud but now up to speed on the treasure hunt, he began to take interest in the items we had not yet found. And that's when he learned about the skull.

"I've seen one," he confided to us.

"What do you mean?"

"I mean, I've seen one! Okay, I haven't actually seen it. But I've heard about it. A skull. Just like what Walt's talking about. It has to be what he wants. It's on a stick in the middle of a square in this little town in Peru. Just a skull and a few statues. I can get it for him. I know I can. Let me try."

***

He tried and failed. Based on something his wife told him about ruins outside the Peruvian city of Cuzco, Declan concluded that the skull Walt needed was that of an ancient sports hero ("the Michael Jordan of the Incas!") that the natives paraded around during special ceremonies. He believed it was still there, on a stick, in a historical site called Sacsayhuaman. All he needed to do to get it was fly down there and walk off with it in the middle of the night.

Tommy Goode volunteered to go with him. Tommy went based on a misunderstanding, having heard the name of the ruins pronounced as Sexy Woman and thinking he would get to raid some thousand-year-old sorority. But in the end he turned out to be helpful anyway. When the two of them couldn't get to the dig site after sunset, they returned during the day and were confronted by a security force that kept the boys on a tight leash as they tried to get access to a vault full of mummies. Things were looking hopeless until Tommy had an idea: one of the security guards was a woman and he would use his considerable charm to enlist her as an ally.

With anyone else the idea would have been crazy but Tommy's ability to court women was legendary. With his Elvis looks and devilish smile he could have talked Mother Theresa into joining an all-girl rock band, so he figured that converting some Andean honey would be no problem. He got the security guard alone, told her what he wanted to do, and confidently asked for her help.

The woman took all of two seconds to think about it. Then she blew her whistle and the entire guard corps swooped down and spirited Tommy out of the site faster than he could say Alberto Fujimori.

Left alone, Declan was able to dash into the burial chamber and throw a poncho over his intended target. While Tommy was getting the third-degree, Declan and the skull got away unscathed.

Unfortunately the chamber was dark and Declan was in a hurry. Instead of Michael Jordan's skull, by mistake he grabbed a horse's head kept in honor of a cavalry charge that saved the Spanish from an Incan massacre in 1532. It was a skull alright, and it was in pristine condition. But it was not at all what Walt was seeking. When they showed it to Walt back in Panama he promptly sent them back out on the road for another attempt.

***

The Puyo and Sacsayhuaman incidents misled Walt into thinking that the skull he wanted was somewhere in the mountains.

At first Declan agreed. Though he was wrong about Sacsayhuaman, he stayed committed to the Andes and spent months looking there for a clue that matched the image he had of a head on a stick. Much of that time was spent flying around in the C-27 but he also made trips on his own dime to lesser-known places like Tarahuasi, Abancay, and Kotosh, often dragging his wife along and making her stay in middle-of-nowhere hotels that it's safe to say she never would have seen otherwise in a hundred years. For people who didn't explore, the two began to enjoy the adventure. They visited half the Peruvian range and became veritable experts on Incan archeology.

But their frustration grew with each failed search. One day, after a grueling hike through the thin air of Machu Picchu, Sue collapsed on a bench and commented that if they hadn't found it by now, there was no way the skull was within a thousand miles.

And so Declan had his epiphany. He realized then that what Walt wanted lay not in the highlands at all but hundreds of miles away in the place where no one was looking: the jungle.

He therefore volunteered for a hub-and-spoke in Iquitos, a town so remote in eastern Peru that no roads even went there. You needed a plane or a boat to reach it. Our squadron would often base a crew and one C-27 there for weeks at a time in order to supply Peruvian troops who guarded the border with Brazil. Declan had never volunteered for that mission in the past. He usually avoided those long assignments because his wife abhorred the three-week absence. But the more the skull eluded him the more determined he was to find it. Tommy went with him again and I tagged along as a third wheel.

***

To date, nobody had found anything in Iquitos that was even remotely connected to Walt's dream. That struck everyone as odd because

Iquitos was *the* launching point for Amazon exploration and because so much of what Walt envisioned seemed to come from that mother of all jungles.

But where in Iquitos? I assumed that when we got there we would start where we always started when we needed information: with Jaime, a Spanish immigrant who ran a quiet restaurant and seemed to know everything that was going on.

Tommy disagreed, arguing that we should go right to the seamy side of life and ask the street kids and the prostitutes. "If we want a skull," he argued, "chances are they know where all the bodies are hidden." But Declan, as always, had his own take on the situation. The man he wanted to talk to was Juan Maldonado.

Maldonado was key because Iquitos, though in the jungle, wasn't the jungle itself. It was a fortress of humanity surrounded by an oasis of jungle. Few people ever went beyond the walls. Maldonado was one of the few.

***

"He's still got the flies," Tommy observed as we sat at a table at Ari's Burger and watched Juan work the sidewalk.

"He does indeed," Declan agreed.

Ari's Burger was an open air cafeteria in the center of Iquitos right on the Plaza de Armas. The plaza was always filled with pedestrian traffic. Juan, in his oversized clothes and floppy hat, was a sidewalk salesman whose job was to get customers into Ari's.

He approached passersby with a friendly greeting and ingratiating wave of a hand and talked them into stopping for a bite. If one person turned him down, he turned immediately to the next. The only time

Juan stood still was when no prospects headed his way. When that happened, he backed into the shade of the restaurant's awning and waited. Even then his eyes stayed in motion, looking down the sidewalk, across the square, or up the street. The flies, too, never stopped circling his canvas hat. There were always a dozen buzzing around his head regardless of the weather or time of day. It was hard not to look at him without thinking he was a dizzy cartoon character.

"You really think he knows something about skulls?" Tommy asked doubtfully.

"If he doesn't, I don't know who else we could ask."

"What about the kids?"

"I checked. A few bodies, but no skulls."

"What about Jaime?"

"No," I said.

"Nothing?"

I thought back to the night before when Declan and I stopped by Jaime's place to pose the same question. It wasn't his verbal response that stuck in my mind, a blunt *No* flavored with the distaste that only centuries of aristocratic breeding can distill. It was more the look that told me what un-incarcerated barbarians he thought us to be.

"Nothing," I confirmed.

Eventually Juan took a break. He shepherded one last couple into the cafe and then tucked himself away at a table in the corner, dining on chicken and fried rice a waitress brought him as pay. The three of us crossed the restaurant to join him.

"Hola, Juan."

"Hola, amigos!" he greeted us, his smile a dentist's nightmare. His voice was squeaky and slipped across his errant teeth like a weak wave crossing scattered rocks. *"Qué tal con la fuerza aérea?"*

"Muy bien," I told him. "We can't complain. We are here in Iquitos, the jewel of the Amazon. Life is good."

"Sí," he agreed, happy to have company. "Would you like to buy an ocelot?"

"Señor, what would I do with an ocelot?"

"He would be a wonderful pet for you. I can get you one for one hundred dollars."

"I already know a man who can get me a jaguar for fifty."

"Then I can get you an ocelot for fifty dollars. You do not want a jaguar. They are mean."

"And an ocelot is not mean?"

"Not this one. She is a beautiful baby."

"Thank you, *señor*, but I think I will not buy an ocelot today."

"How about a crocodile?"

"No, thank you. However, I do have a question for you. We are interested in…"

He slapped the table. "You are young men! Full of energy! If you are here in two weeks I can offer you Juan Maldonado's jungle survival course. Two hundred dollars apiece. I have trained many soldiers and I can train you. When you are finished you will know how to live in the jungle like a native."

"How long is the course?" I couldn't help asking.

"Five days. Just you and your friends and me. All you take with you is a machete but I will teach you to survive all the same." He made a slashing motion. "There is no problem in the jungle you cannot fix with a machete."

"Where did you learn to survive in the jungle?"

"Ha! I learned the hard way. I had to learn because I was lost. I have friends there. *Indios*. They taught me the old ways. It is a good thing, too, or Juan Maldonado would not be here today."

"Indians saved your life?" I asked.

"They did."

"But I thought they tried to kill you," I said, remembering a story Josh had told me.

"Some Indians tried to kill me," Juan agreed, a pained look coming to his face. His voice softened and the words slurred even more through his teeth. "But I hid. I hid and I did not move and they never found me. Then I tried to come home, come back to Iquitos, but I became lost and thought I would never leave the jungle alive. The jungle will crush you if you let her! Crush you and pick you apart piece by piece until there is nothing, not even your bones. But my friends the Witato found me and ever since I have known how to live with the jungle."

"Is that when you picked up the flies?" Tommy asked before I could shush him.

"What flies?" Juan asked.

Declan interrupted just then to demand a translation. I explained the conversation thus far while simultaneously kicking Tommy under the table.

"Juan," I began, ignoring a fly that spun from its orbit around Juan's hat and landed on my hand, "it is because you are such an expert in the jungle that I want to ask you a question. We need the help of someone with your experience." Briefly I explained our situation, keeping the story of our treasure hunt short for fear he would think we were nuts. I didn't want a man with flies to think I was nuts.

"No," he said when I finished, not even looking up from his food.

"You can't help us?"

"No," he repeated. "I cannot."

Tommy and I slumped in our chairs. Only Declan, who couldn't follow the conversation and had to go on facial cues alone, stayed interested.

"He's lying," he announced.

"Why do you think that?"

"Trust me. He knows something. Convince him we're not doing this for kicks. There's a skull out here with a story and he knows where it is."

Declan was earnest so I sat up and tried again. This time I went for broke and told Juan about Walt's dream, the other items on the list, Declan's trip to Cuzco, and how we had come to believe that somehow Iquitos was involved. I laid bare our meager souls to a man with flies.

Juan ate as I rambled, devouring his meal and then looking around for more. Tommy winked at a waitress and ordered another plate of chicken and rice. Juan polished that off, too, not interrupting me but not seeming to pay much attention, either. When he finished eating, I expected him to repeat his earlier answer but he didn't. Instead he wiped his mouth on his sleeve and stared at the tabletop.

"Your friend is here?" he said.

"No," I replied. "Walt did not come on this trip. He sent us in his place."

"He believes this dream?"

"With all his heart. He has thought of nothing else for a year."

"And what does he think it means?"

I asked the others for help with that one. I wasn't sure what *I* thought of Walt's dream and didn't feel qualified to speak for him. Tommy and Declan weighed in. After much discussion I went with a variation of what Declan had just said.

"We don't know, Juan, but we think it's about stories," I admitted. "*Cuentos*. There are stories down here in the jungle that are waiting to be told. Walt's dream is telling him not to let them go by."

Juan smacked his lips and thought about that. He was a short man and as he thought he shrank into his clothes.

"It is not close," he said, making up his mind. He took a pencil from a waitress and scrawled a crude map on a napkin, slowly and with great concentration printing in block letters the names of rivers next to the lines. "Half a day on a boat, then a walk. But I know what you want. I know where is your skull."

We sat up in our seats.

"This is a human skull?" Tommy clarified with a glance at Declan. *"No queremos otra cabeza de caballo."*

Juan's lips parted but not in a smile. In his tooth-deficient way he grimaced.

"These are not the heads of horses I will take you to see," he promised. "They are human and they are real."

"How can you be sure?"

"Because I knew the men they belonged to."

***

Josh had heard a story about Juan working for a mine in the jungle, one that was overrun by hostile Indians. I never asked him where that story originated. So many stories from the jungle depend on who you hear them from, how many times that person has told the tale, and whether anyone is around to corroborate the events. Juan told a much different story as we left the docks the next morning. It turned out he liked to talk. He did both in a rust-bucket riverboat with two smoking diesel engines.

"Your friend wants to know the stories of this land," he began in a voice just audible over the motors. He sat on a gunwale and motioned for us to sit beside him. "*Bueno*. Here is a story for you."

As we chugged east down the Amazon, Juan told us the tale of the Iquito.

For as long as anyone knew, the four major tribes of the area were the Iquito, the Witato, the Yaguar, and the Bora.

All four tribes were hunter-gatherers. They had lived on this stretch of the Amazon since time immemorial, fighting amongst themselves but abiding by an unspoken understanding that everyone belonged to the land. What distinguished one tribe from another was only their clannish structure – that and a tribe-centric conviction that each was first among equals.

The Yaguar and the Bora were fishermen. The Iquito and the Witato were hunters. The Yaguar and the Bora had the most constant supply of food – they prospered with the largest settlements. The Iquito and the Witato, on the other hand, went through cycles of surplus and want, and their villages were smaller and more dispersed.

This disparity in fortune caused friction particularly because it was the Iquito and Witato who always took the lead to fight off interlopers who tried to move into the region. The Yaguar and the Bora supported their neighbors with food and tools during these struggles but it was the hunters who bore the brunt of combat and felt themselves to be more responsible for the land. The division of duties, too, forged a closer bond between the Iquito and the Witato than between them and the other tribes. The fishermen were soft, prone to trade and outside influence, whereas the Iquito and the Witato – but especially the Iquito – worked to stay aloof and maintain their identity. They fought from time to time but understood that in the face of determined opposition they could always count on each other.

So things continued for hundreds, even thousands of years, Juan told us.

When the first white men arrived, missionaries, things changed. The Jesuits came from Spain and brought god and empire with them. They were followed by the Portuguese and then the English and the *norteamericanos*. They were also followed by soldiers and then by traders and miners and loggers and settlers. Always there were more settlers. Always there were more outsiders, *cohuori*, who told the Four Tribes how they needed to change, how they needed to live, and how they needed to move off land that the newer people wanted. The tribes became sick. Many died. Their cultures weakened and so did their resistance. The hunting lands of the Iquito and the Witato shrank. The best fishing site of the Yaguar and the Bora, at the long bend of the Great River above the Rio Nanay, became a port and then a village. The Spanish called the village Iquitos, after the Indians who hunted there. It grew and became a village that other settlers came to from far away, traveling up the Great River in boats.

The *cohuori* brought schools and religions and new ways of living. They bred with the tribes, mixing the bloodlines and weakening the identity of who was Bora, for example, and who was something else. Almost everyone in Iquitos has native blood in them, Juan noted, but few know what it is or which tribe it came from.

Most of the Yaguar and the Bora ceased fishing and moved into Iquitos. Many Witato also gave in. The Shipibo, late arrivals to the area, abandoned the jungle altogether and sold arts and crafts in the town squares. Only the Iquito held out. Entering the 20th century they were the last true *indios* of the original tribes, refusing to intermarry, continuing their hunter-gatherer ways, and dwindling in their shrinking habitat. Eventually they stopped being seen at all. Everyone assumed they had died out.

***

Juan told us this much and then his voice trailed off. Our boatman steered us to the center of the river where the current was the strongest but the water less choppy. Twice one of the engines failed, seizing with such violence that the whole boat shook and expelled a cloud of black smoke like an eruption from our hold. Each time the boatman got it running again. His name was Old Feo and though he was neither old nor ugly he moved about the decks of his battered craft like a seasoned sailor.

"Sooooo," said Declan, stretching his legs. "What does any of that have to do with skulls?"

Juan watched the shore slide past like it was a favorite movie. As he often did, he seemed not to pay attention.

"I was fourteen years old," he continued, his voice stronger as he moved from the distant past to his own lifetime. Doing quick math I decided that meant it was the early 1950s. "I was tired of shining shoes and wanted a better job. Some people from the capital came into town, government people. They had plans *de desarollo*, of development. We had the land from Ecuador in the war and the president wanted to develop it. There was oil, they said, and gold and copper. There would be rubber again, and they would fish the rivers to export around the world. There were medicines in the forest, and trees, and exotic animals to send to zoos. These men came and went off in all directions to make their plans..."

A patch of giant water lilies floated past the starboard side. Some were big enough to support a goat.

"Those men," Tommy prompted. "Did you go with them?"

"*Sí*. They needed boys to carry bags and clean up. I work hard so they took me along."

"Where did you go?"

He pointed past our bow. "The Río Nanay," he answered.

"Why did they want to go there?"

"That was their destination. Other groups went to other regions, into other rivers. We went to the Nanay. They said it was valuable, that the river had things they could study and use. I think they wanted the trees. There were great trees on the Nanay, tall cedar that they could saw into planks and float down the river. One man, all he could talk about was lumber. But we never got that far."

Old Feo moved us out of the middle to avoid a sandbar and thereafter stuck close to the north bank. That put us close to the jungle and the brooding shadows of the trees.

"What did you find in the Nanay?" I asked.

"We found trouble," Juan said. "Two days out of Iquitos we found trouble. You see, the Nanay was the last place to find the Iquito Indians. They were untouched by the *cohuori* and they wanted to stay that way. They were wild and angry – and good with poison darts," he emphasized.

"Like the Korubo," I suggested.

"The Korubo are not real," Juan shook his head. "The Iquito were real. They lived on the Nanay. It is their river and it has always protected them. The forests are thick, there are piranha in the water that will strip a man to the bone, and quicksand is on the shore. It is wild and angry like them. For that reason the Iquito lived on the Nanay."

"And?"

"And two nights after we arrived they attacked our camp."

He stopped talking then. No amount of questioning encouraged him to continue.

We rode in silence until reaching the mouth of the Nanay River. Old Feo pointed us into the new current. He wasn't a great talker, either, though in his case it seemed to be less bottled-up trauma than personality that made him that way. He just didn't have a lot to say. Except for commenting on the sandbars and muttering over the engines, he stood by the tiller and kept his thoughts to himself, a New World Charon unfazed by our destination. His one deviation was when Tommy hopped up onto the gunwale to peer over the side, musing on the piranha. Old Feo advised simply, "Don't fall in."

Two hours up the Nanay, Juan raised his hand and Old Feo hove to. We stopped on the north bank of an oxbow where the water curled back on itself and created a still pool. Juan scanned the tree line.

"What are we looking for?" Tommy asked.

"Sendero," Juan replied.

"Why do we need a trail? I thought you were attacked on the river."

Juan kept his eyes on the shore and motioned Old Feo to move us forward. After several yards he pointed.

"Allá." Old Feo chopped the power and turned right, letting momentum push us between the trees. Around us great roots rose and fell across the surface. Patches of sand appeared but drifted too lightly in the water to be stable. The hull floated between both as though on a secret channel. When it finally bumped against the bottom we were close enough to dry ground to hop ashore. Juan stood up.

"We were attacked on the shore," he confirmed. "But the shore now is not where it was forty years ago. The river has moved and that place is gone. Now it sits on a marsh and we are not going there."

"Then where are we going?" Declan wanted to know.

Juan understood his question before I could translate.

"You want to go where the skulls are. They are not on the river. They are with their new owners."

"And who's that?"

"The Iquito. We go to their village."

***

There was no trail, not for a while. Where we hopped off the boat was simply a spot Juan recognized. From there he and his machete led us through choking brush until intercepting a path two hundred yards on.

Tommy, Declan, and I would have been lost within minutes but Juan never hesitated. When I asked how he navigated, he said that instead of trying to find the way by looking at the ground – as we did – he looked up and watched the trees. He sauntered through the forest with his head held high, noting certain trees the way one glances at a highlighted page.

We trekked for an hour, covering maybe two miles. While we walked I drank both my canteens and ate the sandwich I had tucked into a pocket for lunch. The water I sweated back out by the time Juan stopped and motioned for us to gather round.

"We are close," he said, pointing ahead as though we could see anything except more jungle, which we couldn't.

"Close to what?" Tommy asked. "The Iquito village? You said they don't exist anymore."

Juan shook his head. "I said that people believed the Iquito were no more," he corrected. "But when the government people came and explored the area, we learned that the Iquito were still here. In small numbers, but they were here."

"And they attacked your party?" Declan wanted to know. "They killed all your expedition people and cut off their heads, is that what happened?"

Juan removed his hat. When he did his flies seemed confused over whether they should follow the hat or stay by his head: they broke from their orbits and buzzed chaotically around all of us until Juan put it back on.

"No, they didn't kill anyone," he replied as though thinking about it for the first time. "The Iquito attacked and hurt several men but everyone escaped that day. Everyone except for me," he smiled ruefully. "I was gathering firewood and they left me behind."

"No!"

"*Sí.*"

"What did you do?"

"I hid. I hid in a marsh near the river and stayed there two days until I was sure no one was around. The smell was horrible. I was wet and cold and afraid that I would be eaten by a snake. Then I tried to walk home, back to Iquitos. I wanted to go into the river but I cannot swim so I tried to follow it upstream. But even that was not easy. I did not know how to walk in the jungle so soon I lost even the river." He laughed. "Now I think it is funny that one can lose a river but yes, it is true. One can."

"How did you survive?" I asked.

"After two days more I had eaten only snails and some bird eggs. I no longer knew where I was. I ate some berries and my eyesight became bad. Never do that, my friends. Never eat berries in the jungle. I was hungry, alone, and quite ill – I was sure I would die. Then one afternoon I looked up and three men stood near me. They were

Witato. In my wanderings I had gone north, away from the river and closer to their territory. They took me in and saved my life."

"Wow!" said Declan. "What luck! But why didn't they kill you?"

"Why would they kill me?"

"I don't know. Why not?"

Juan shook his head. "No one kills just because. Not here. Not even the Iquito. The Witato did not kill me. I stayed with them a year before returning to Iquitos."

He described living with the Witato in a *malocca* on the Río Momón. He shared a home with Onao, one of the men who found him, and with Onao's son, Oten. In the end, the only reason he returned to town was because more of the tribe was moving there and they asked him to help them make the transition. He began to explain some kind of business relationship he had with them starting in the early sixties but Declan looked at his watch and interrupted.

"Mike, this is all interesting but the day's not getting any younger. What are we doing about the skull?"

I relayed Declan's impatience to Juan, who nodded and motioned for us to follow. He pushed his way up the trail where the air brightened. Minutes later we broke into a clearing.

Before us was a stretch of ground of maybe twenty acres. High grass and brush covered it but there were no trees. The area had been clear-cut.

"What happened here?" Tommy asked.

"Loggers," Juan replied. "Teak and mahogany. This has all been cut in the last five years. All the trees are gone."

All the trees were gone but the clearing wasn't scraped bare. The jungle was already fighting to take back the land. In five years it had covered the area in new growth several feet deep. Unfortunately it would take hundreds of years to regain the trees. That was the big shock the area afforded: bursting from the lushness of the jungle into a comparative moonscape, we didn't have to be forest rangers to know that something was wrong.

"Loggers did this?" Declan repeated. He turned to look behind us at the jungle, amazed at the difference.

"How did they get the trees out of here?" Tommy wondered, but no sooner were the words out of his mouth than we noticed a feeder river on the east side of the clearing. Juan confirmed that it ran east into the Nanay.

"There, you have seen it. Now we go to the village," he said, and turned us back down the trail.

"We're not near the village now?"

"No. It is back on the river."

"Then why did we come up here?" I asked.

He pointed at the clearing. "I am telling you a story, *señores*. This part of it you had to see with your own eyes."

On the way back down the trail I asked Juan if he ever again ran into the Iquito who attacked his party that day when he was fourteen. He was too busy listening to the forest and watching the trees to answer me then, but as we neared the river he pulled up and gathered us round.

"*Sí*," he said. "When I lived with the Witato they sometimes met with the Iquito their neighbors. In those days they were still friendly to each other."

"They're not now?"

Juan wagged his head left and right, not saying yes or no.

"Many of the Witato – *bueno*, most of them – have moved into town. Some Iquito have followed but only a few. There are now Witato on the Momón and Iquito on the Nanay, but the Witato have close relations with their brothers and sisters in Iquitos. The Iquito, no. If you are Iquito and you leave, you are gone."

"So the Witato out here are more modern than the Iquito?" Tommy clarified. "Do they still get along then?"

Juan sighed, frustrated. He wasn't an educated man to begin with. Now he was trying to give us a short course in the anthropology of four cultures and it wasn't going well.

"Once," he tried, "we could speak of 'the Witato' or 'the Bora' and mean everyone in the tribe. Now those identities are in pieces. There are Witato who get their shoes shined on the *Malecón*. There are others *en la selva* who have never worn shoes. The same is true for the other tribes, except for the Iquito. Of all people, the Iquito defend their history and their land. The Iquito here are pure – they have tools and guns, but if they are here they do not intermarry and they still rely on the jungle. You must understand that before we go to the village."

"Why?"

"Because five years ago some Witato made an arrangement with loggers. There is much demand in Colombia for expensive wood. Companies hire people to come to our land and find the best trees. My friend Oten and others allowed a company to cut down a stand of mahogany on Witato land..." – he pointed back up the trail. "But there is no such thing as Witato land. Oten was a good man but he had moved to town. Even other Witato were not happy with what he did. Worse, the loggers encountered the Iquito and shot one of them."

"Oh-oh," said Tommy.

"*Sí*. Three years ago, after the trees were gone, after the Colombians were gone, after the government ignored Iquito complaints, Oten and four partners went to the Nanay to seek other areas to log. They were killed by Iquito. The Iquito cut off their heads and mounted them on stakes where the mahogany forest had stood. Later they took the heads to their village. That is where they are now, and that is where we go."

He told us this with no apparent bitterness, only the grimace that was doubly painful with its missing teeth. We listened in horror.

"Your friend?" Declan exclaimed when I translated.

Juan nodded inside his floppy hat. He prepared to move on but Tommy stopped him.

"Hold on, Juan. What did the Witato do? Are the tribes at war now?"

Juan unslung his machete and chopped free a water leanna hanging nearby. He gulped the liquid inside until the vine was empty.

"No. There was an investigation. This time the government sent an agent and identified the killers. The Iquito did not hide what they had done and there was no reason for them to. It is not like in *el Ecuador* where tribes are autonomous, but still in Peru they make their own decisions and pass their own judgments. The tribes met. They decided that the killers were wrong but Oten was wrong, too. There is now peace but relations are no longer what they were. The Iquito have refused to return the heads to Oten's tribe. They are still angry and it has been three years."

We walked to the river and boarded the boat, where Old Feo stood in the same place as when we had left him. As he cast off, I tried to sum up the situation thus far.

"So, Juan. We're about to visit a bunch of people who once tried to kill you, who killed some of your friends and still have their heads, and who are angry about something that happened five years ago. Is that right?"

Juan nodded. I felt ill. Declan looked like he regretted ever getting involved in Walt's search. Only Tommy was relaxed. He propped his feet on the gunwale and slapped Declan encouragingly on the back.

"It could be worse," he told us. "They could all be homos. Hey Juan, tell me about Iquito women."

***

The Iquito village was really three settlements within a half-mile of each other further up the Nanay. Whatever I expected, they underwhelmed.

First, they were quiet. Each clearing held a dozen huts with bamboo walls but no more than that many people were about and those were mostly women. Second, while we did see a wooden cayuca there were also two flat-bottomed metal bass boats pulled onto the shore. The way Juan had been throwing around the word 'pure' in referring to the Iquito, I envisioned them being Stone Age denizens dragged reluctantly into the light. Not hardly. The third revelation reinforced the second: the men who came to greet us all wore shorts. Cotton shorts cut off at the knees. Being pure looked pretty modern.

We bypassed the first settlement and pulled to shore at the second. Three men met us, wandering over from a fire where they were burning trash. They were a deeper brown than Juan, lithe, and walked with a subtle bow-legged gate. Except for wide ear holes and the shorts, any of them could have passed for someone in the Plaza de Armas.

Juan spoke to them in their language. We listened. Declan relaxed when the men didn't act hostile. I didn't relax but tried to look like this was all familiar, like I had once dealt with headhunters back on the South Side of Chicago and meeting them again here was no big thing. Tommy focused on the women.

Juan turned back to us.

"Tibau Oma is a clan leader," he told us, gesturing to an Indian who had to be sixty years old. "These are his sons. Tibau said if you want to see the skulls you can."

"Do they speak Spanish?" I asked.

"No. They would not speak it to you even if they could."

"So much for persuading them," Tommy muttered, reading my mind.

"Juan," I said. "Did you tell them why we are interested in the skulls?"

"Not yet."

"But what have you been talking about for ten minutes?"

Juan thought about that, perhaps pondering why gringos are always in a hurry. There I was, anxious to get on to what I was interested in, while he was reestablishing a relationship with people he saw only rarely. Not to mention catching up on clan news.

"The hunting is not good this year," he replied. "The Iquito traditionally hunt to the west, but now they go north to push back the Witato. They believe that if the Witato had not been so close they never would have been tempted to cut down Iquito forests. But Tibau Oma is weary of the constant conflict. He wants to return to their old lands. Also, some men have become frustrated and gone further into the forest. Now the tribe has too many women."

Tommy grunted in approval.

Juan and the men talked some more. Then with no preamble they turned and moved up into the clearing. Whatever relationship they had wasn't warm but it wasn't antagonistic, either. The men seemed familiar with Juan. For his part, he was being more serious than the Juan we were used to. In town and on the boat he projected a simple demeanor. "That's just Juan," was how people at Ari's Burger dismissed him. But here in the village of the Iquito he was solemn and competent. His voice even deepened.

Tibau led us up and around the huts. The clearing there was scattered with tools and fire pits. Far in the back was an overturned cayuca in the process of being resined with breu tree bark. Before the boat was a sight none of us had ever seen and one I would be happy never to observe again. Five chest-high mahogany stakes stuck up from the ground, each sporting a human skull. Some still sported hair.

"Ohhh..." Declan spun on his heel and walked away.

Tibau launched into a peroration. He spoke for fifteen minutes, occasionally supported by murmurs of agreement from his sons. When he was done, Juan turned and with a deadpan face related much the same story he had already told us about the events leading up to Oten's killing. The only variation was Tibau's insistence that Oten was being paid not just for the cutting rights but as part of a deliberate effort by outside parties to intrude on Iquito land and diminish their influence. That the Witato would profit at the Iquito's expense was all part of the plan.

"Do you agree with that?" I asked Juan when he finished.

With his back to the Iquito, Juan allowed himself a small roll of the eyes.

"Oten was not thinking like a Witato when he let them cut down the trees," he said. "He had no plan other than to make money for his family."

"Well, it sounds like they're settling in to a stalemate," Tommy remarked. "But maybe they'll get over it in time. Say, Juan, do any of these girls go around topless? That one back there was really cute but she was wearing a shirt."

"They are not getting over it," Juan disagreed. "I know Iquito. Nothing has changed in their feelings for the land. When it comes to protecting it, they are...*despiadado.*"

"Ruthless," I translated. "Obviously. But Juan, if nothing has changed then what are we doing here?"

He waved his hand to indicate I had misunderstood. "They will protect their land," he said, "but there is room for compromise with the Witato. I believe Tibau would like a reason to put this incident behind him. But for now there is no reason, and that is unfortunate because the tribes would carry more influence if they worked together."

"How so?"

"Like those men years ago," he explained, "there are still people who wish to develop this region. Oten was not the only one to cut down trees. The hunting grounds for both tribes have decreased. The Iquito now push into Witato land so the Witato look around for something else. There are also Yaguar who wish to bring tourists here, and Bora who still fish, and others who talk of mining the rivers. The tribes can unite and resist these pressures but ever since the killings they do not. They look out for themselves. Even the Yaguar and the Bora refuse to join with them to lobby the government."

"But the Yaguar and the Bora...they get along, right?"

"Well, that is difficult, too. The Bora have a dispute with the Witato because the Witato fish now that their hunting lands have decreased. And the Bora and Yaguar argue over things on shore. *Pues*, the Bora feel pressured from two sides."

I motioned to Tommy. He and I huddled. Just what were we supposed to do?

Tommy had no idea.

"Juan," I cleared my throat. "Would you explain to Tibau that we have no desire to cut down trees? Tell him you have told us the story of the Iquito and we have the greatest respect for his tribe."

Tommy asked what I was doing.

"Stalling," I said. "I don't know what else to say. For all I know these guys think we're loggers."

When Juan finished relaying the message he turned back to me expecting more. At that point I was stuck. If the Witato couldn't get the skulls back, how could I ask for them? And forget convincing Tibau, how could I convince myself to steal one away just to put it on Walt's shelf?

Declan returned then, looking pale. He stood near Tommy.

"I found a woman for you," he whispered.

"Really?" Tommy's eyes lit up. "Which one? The girl with the boobs?"

"Uh-huh. I puked and she cleaned it up. Any woman who does that is a keeper."

"Declan," I interrupted. "What should we do? These guys are still mad at the Witato, and as long as they keep these heads the Witato are mad at them. And what do we want? Help, I'm lost here."

Declan clenched his jaw and forced himself to look at the heads, from the small one with the broken teeth all the way over to the skull that had to belong to Oten, the one with the long hair and a prominent position to the front of the group.

"Give Tibau the dream speech," he ordered.

"The what?"

"The dream speech. Let's stitch this up. Link what we want with what he wants. Come on, these people have been hunting together for centuries: he doesn't want to be mad at the Witato. And the Witato probably don't want to be mad at them. Tell this guy about Walt's dream. Tell him that Walt is being guided to fix things up, to bring people together who shouldn't be fighting. What better way than to give us the skulls and let *us* take them to the Witato. He can save face and still do a good thing, and all the tribes will be better off."

"You have a career ahead of you in politics," I told him.

"Whatever. Just so long as I don't have to touch those things. What a bunch of savages. I'm going to puke again just looking at them."

***

Tibau didn't give us the skulls. He did agree to consider Declan's proposal, however, and told us to return in two days. We went back to Iquitos empty-handed.

Two days later the Air Operations Center in Panama called down with a series of taskings, interrupting our trip back to the Iquito. I volunteered to travel upriver with Juan while Declan and Tommy flew out to the radar sites but Declan wouldn't hear of it. He smelled negotiation in the air. Notwithstanding his almost non-existent Spanish, he demanded to go back for the skulls.

So Tommy and I flew all day between Sites 5 and 8. We didn't return until sunset. When we did, Declan was nowhere to be found. Neither was Juan.

At six the next morning when we left for the airport, Declan still hadn't returned to the hotel. I found one of the street kids, Tonio, and asked him to find out what he could.

That night we landed after dark. We went directly to Ari's Burger where Tonio greeted us with aplomb.

"You didn't tell me he had left town," he accused us.

"You claim to know everything," I replied. "I didn't know I had to help you with the basics."

"You don't need to help me. I can find out anything about anyone."

"Prove it. Where is Declan?"

"Ten soles."

"I'm not giving you ten soles."

"Okay, then I shine your shoes?"

While he polished our sneakers to a fine brown gloss, Tonio informed us that Declan had spent the previous night in the Iquito village on the Nanay. He had returned to town in the afternoon but then left again. He and Juan were last seen at a settlement about five miles upstream from the *Malecón*.

"Upstream? Who lives there?" Tommy asked.

"Bora," Tonio replied. He spat in disgust.

"You don't like Bora?"

As reply, he sniffed his armpit. "They stink," he said.

The next day we flew again to Site 8, taking scaffolding that came into Iquitos on a DHL flight and that took forever to transload between the two planes. The troops at 8 wanted to build a watch tower – the radar worked well for distant targets but it had too many blind spots in the near regions that they could cover simply with a man with binoculars. We returned by mid-afternoon but it wasn't until nine o'clock that night that Declan knocked on my door.

"Dude, we were getting worried," I told him.

"I paid Tonio to tell you where I was," he replied.

"*You* paid him? We paid him to find you."

"He didn't have to find me. I borrowed one of his little pals to be my translator so he knew where I was the whole time. The shyster."

"You took a kid with you? Up the river?"

"Yeah. I didn't start out with him but after ten minutes of interpretive dance with Juan I realized there was no way I would be able to communicate with anybody without someone who spoke English. Tonio knew a rug rat at the docks who learned English from the SEALs and set me up with him. The kid swears a lot but otherwise is good."

"But what if you had run into trouble?"

"From what?"

"From people who want to cut your head off."

"I would have offered them a nine-year-old brat. They could cut his head off. He's a street kid, nobody would miss him."

Tommy came in with beer but Declan waved him away.

"No booze. I've got the runs," he explained. "We spent last night with some Bora family up past that old shipwreck on the sandbar. It's not far but it's light-years from here in all the ways that count. Electricity, for one. Food for another. I don't even know what I ate for dinner last night. Roast tarantula, probably. For a few hours I thought I might have caught whatever you had last year, Mike..."

"Don't remind me."

"...but that's okay because the malaria I got from the mosquitoes will kill whatever's in my stomach."

"What were you doing talking to the Bora? You were supposed to be taking the heads to the Witato."

"Oh, no. No, my friends, it couldn't possibly be that easy. You know, Juan goes on about how pure all these jungle dwellers are but when it comes right down to it, they're a bunch of opportunistic bastards. Heartless, too. A cross between the mob and the insurance industry." Declan tried to look angry but there was satisfaction in his tone. "We went to the Witato. I had Juan give the dream speech again. They bought into it so I thought, great, we're good to go. The Iquito are willing to deal, the Witato are willing to deal – everyone's happy. But then Juan mentioned that we want one of the skulls to take back to Walt…"

"Just like that?" I asked.

"Just like that. Well, naturally their antennae go up. I want to do *what*? One of Oten's brothers was there and he practically fell off his chair, he was so angry. I got worried then. If people down here chop the heads off loggers, what do they do to grave robbers? But it didn't get that bad. Believe it or not, some of the others were amenable to the idea. Of course, the brother was dead-set against. So they started this big discussion that lasted all afternoon and into the night. We ended up staying out there until morning."

"What was that like?"

"Camping. Camping in the jungle with a million bugs. Lots of stars, though."

"Any women?" Tommy asked. Declan ignored him.

"So," he continued. "The next morning, the brother – he had some weird name but I call him Otto – had a complete change of tune. He came to me with a proposal: Otto said that since I have such an interest in tribal harmony, he wants me to look into a beef the Witato have with the Bora. It seems the Witato fish in Bora waters, so if I can get the Bora to stop complaining then he might see his way to letting me borrow his brother's skull."

"You know," Tommy observed, "as sentences go, that's got to be one of the weirdest ones I've ever heard."

"Forget the sentence. It's one of the weirdest *offers* I've ever heard. The night before, the guy thought I was a sicko for wanting his brother's head. Now all of a sudden he's like, okay, you can have it but only if you talk these other guys out of my favorite fishing hole. What's that?"

"What did you say?"

"What could I say? I told him I would look into it. And in all honesty, it's a serious issue. No Witato or Bora have killed each other yet but there have been fights out on the river. The other members of the tribe convinced Otto that the last thing they need is more Witato dead and stuck on pikes. Not that the Bora would do that but still... So yesterday Juan and I came back up the river and visited the Bora."

"And they would be who? How would I recognize a Bora if I saw him in the street?"

"You wouldn't. They look like anyone else around here. Except they've got these gypsy-like bands that live outside town who direct the community."

"What do you mean?"

"Well, the Bora are integrated into Iquitos plenty – like I said, you wouldn't know one if you saw him on the street. But they're still a big clan and they take direction from a handful of families who tell everyone else where they can work and what they should be doing to benefit the clan. You know, like 'you guys can work down on the docks and you guys over there can make and sell shoes and you guys who still have your boats can fish.' That kind of thing."

"Kind of like when I was growing up in New Jersey," Tommy offered.

"Yeah. I mean, it doesn't seem criminal but I couldn't help thinking there was a bit of the Godfather about us having to go see this one guy to ask him about the fishing dispute."

"Did Juan know him?"

"Not personally. He knew who he was, though, and he knew a bunch of people in the family out there. They all knew Juan."

"So what did you all decide? Will they stop arguing with the Witato over fishing rights?"

"Arguing? Dude, they've filed a lawsuit."

"What?"

"Yeah, the Bora are hip to modern stuff. They hang onto the clan thing but they have no problem using whatever they can to get their way. Juan says they discovered lawsuits last year and have been filing them left and right ever since. But here's the funny thing: the lawsuits haven't gone anywhere. I mean, it's not like a cop has gone out and subpoenaed Otto. But they're still out there and Otto hates the fact that everyone in Iquitos now thinks that the Witato are fish thieves simply because the Bora are here in force and that's what they claim. The Bora have seized the public relations upper hand."

Tommy held out his bottle and swirled the beer inside. "So," he said. "The Iquito are willing to give up their feud with the Witato. They'll give the heads back and go back to hunting upriver in exchange for the Witato staying away from their trees. The Witato are willing, but before they agree they want you to broker peace between them and the Bora, who are suing to get back their exclusive fishing rights. Is that right?"

"Yup," Declan nodded.

"And did you work all that out?"

Declan regarded him darkly.

"I didn't finish," he enunciated carefully. "Guess who – despite all their tentacles in Iquitos society – has run up against a wall when it comes to the government?"

"Um, the Bora?"

"Duh. All those lawsuits I mentioned? They get filed by lawyers but they get approved by judges – guess who most of the judges are in town?"

"I don't know."

"The Yaguar."

"You're kidding," I said.

Declan smiled in ironic glee. "Nope. I learned all this last night and just stopped at Jaime's to confirm it. Apparently the Yaguar moved into town decades ago and have failed at everything they've tried to do here since, except politics. Politics and motocarros. If you meet a judge or a taxi driver, chances are good he's a Yaguar."

"So?" asked Tommy, confused. "The Yaguar and Bora are old friends. Why would they...?

"Why would they block Bora lawsuits against the Witato?" Declan finished. "Just to poke a finger in their eye. You see, the Bora and Yaguar don't get along any better than anyone else. Remember how the Bora are fighting the Witato over fishing rights? Well, the Bora also control the other end of that business here – they control the port. You can't fish if you don't have a boat, and you can't fish if you can't bring it into port to sell what you catch. Well, as I mentioned, the Yaguar suck at business. They can get their people to vote which is why they have so many minor officials but they can't get them to open a decent restaurant or run a shop. So they want to get into tourism – eco-tours and stuff – otherwise the next generation will still be driving moto-taxis and just as poor as this one. But they can't get past the teamsters union on the port because the Bora have a lock on the river. I guess the Bora aren't above sinking their competitors, by the way," he added in an aside. "Literally."

"But why won't the Bora share?"

"I asked Jaime the same thing. He says part of it comes down to market share. Look at Iquitos: there's almost no money here. The port and the fishing are small already – the Bora need to hold on to what they've got. Just the same as the Iquito and Witato fighting over hunting grounds."

"So much for centuries of cooperation," I commented. "The Bora are pretty greedy.'

"True, but the Yaguar aren't helping. In their own way they're trying to elbow aside their old friends. Not only do they block Bora access to the courts, Jaime says they use the laws to keep the Bora on the defensive. Little things like business permits, restaurant inspections – yeah, Mike, they have those here – and zoning. There's not much investment here so the economy's a zero-sum game. Once you get something, you hold onto it."

Tommy put his beer down and ticked off the disputes on his fingers. "Iquito-Witato, Witato-Bora, Bora-Yaguar,..." he murmured. "So what do the Bora want?"

"The Yaguar to back off," Declan said simply. "They'll let the Witato fish in the Momón – and only in the Momón – if the Yaguar judges put down their pens and quit closing Bora restaurants."

"That's it?" I asked. "Just get the Yaguar judges under control? That should be easy. I'm from Chicago – you slip the judges a little cash and they'll do whatever you want."

"I don't know," Declan replied. "I asked Jaime about that and he thinks the Yaguar won't budge on anything unless they can get some tour boats and access to the ports. Eco-tours are the future and the Yaguar want in."

"Will the Bora share the ports?" I asked.

Declan didn't answer right away. He finally took one of Tommy's beers and went through an elaborate process of popping the top and wiping the mouth clean. Holding it up to the light, he savored his reply as he checked to see if there were any obvious germs lurking behind the label. "Well," he said. "That's the big question. The guy out by the shipwreck has never seen On the Waterfront but the picture he drew for us was similar to that if the Yaguar try to get access to the docks. That said, he doesn't control that part of the Bora community so he referred us to someone else."

"Really?" Tommy asked. "Who?"

Declan smiled. "Funny you should ask, Tommy old boy. It seems the Bora have a bit of a matriarchal system. There are women in the community who carry a lot of weight. In this particular case, there's one who *really* carries a lot of weight. The family who directs the Bora on the docks is headed by a woman named Bora Jan, also known as Big Jane. She makes all the decisions so if there's going to be any detente down there, she'll be the one to approve it."

Tommy regarded Declan with a superbly blank expression. "Your point?" he asked.

"Well, word has it she's hard to deal with."

"Uh-huh."

"Actually, she has a reputation for being a bitch. Juan's afraid of her."

"And?"

"And Jaime delicately described her as a woman of significant heft."

"So what do you want from me?"

Declan shrugged as though it was obvious. "You're the chick magnet," he reminded Tommy. "Tomorrow morning we have to go to the Yaguar and see if they'll play along with this house of cards I'm building. I'll take Mike along for that. But tomorrow night Jaime's getting me a meeting with Big Jane. For that I'll need you. You've got a good record shmoozing the betties – except for that Incan chick, of course."

"That Incan chick met me later for drinks," Tommy pointed out, "and she brought her handcuffs..."

"All the more reason you have to be there tomorrow night." Declan sat back and sipped his beer. When it got down to an inch of liquid at the bottom of the bottle he studied the black flakes floating there.

"We have two more weeks in Iquitos," I mentioned to no one in particular. "There are four tribes fighting each other down here, some of them violently. Do you honestly think we can change that? Maybe we should just look for a skull somewhere else."

Tommy closed his eyes and leaned back in his chair, musing on Big Jane. Declan was absorbed with the dregs of his beer but he heard my question and shook his head to disagree. For a man juggling so many flaming chainsaws, he was remarkably calm.

"There's no problem, Mike," he assured me. "Everyone wants something. I'll figure out what it is."

"If you insist. I'm just saying, there must be other skulls..."

"No."

"What do you mean, no? How can you be sure?"

"Because it all makes sense," he insisted. "Those Witato are who Walt saw. It fits."

I wasn't so sure but didn't pursue the matter. It was so rare to see Declan enthusiastic about something that it would be cruel to burst his bubble.

"Well," I concluded, "even if we fail, at least we got something out of this. We finally found a way to break you out of your shell. You're as happy as a street kid with a bucket of glue being so involved. You even got a few meals out of it. Not to mention some interesting places to spend the night."

Declan belched, poured the rest of his beer into a potted plant, and stood to go. "Yeah," he allowed. "I suppose everyone has a calling. Mine just happens to be decapitated Indians. But as for interesting places..." he wrinkled his nose in disgust. "The first night was okay.

Those houses the Witato have aren't bad. But sleeping out by that shipwreck last night sucked. And..." he wagged a finger at Tommy, "just so you know, the Bora stink."

***

The Yaguar were easy to deal with at first. Declan and I met their representative at an alderman's office on Raimondi Street near the Loreto Plaza. The room was small but opened onto an airy courtyard decorated with *azulejos*, the decorative tiles brought from Portugal during the rubber boom. *Azuelos* can be chic and these were trimmed in a bright, faux-gold design to heighten the modish effect. It lent a snooty atmosphere to the place that was a perfect fit for its occupant. He was Yoni, a skinny man with a round face, a bulb nose, and the easy, calculated speech of a game show host.

The Bora are our friends, Yoni assured us. He promised that if the Yaguar could get a berth or two at the docks – or permission to build new berths – then not only would the Bora see their legal problems vanish, in fact the Yaguar would help them build new restaurants and stores for all the tourists the Yaguar hoped to attract. Yoni was a senior judge in town and he had the influence to make that happen.

"That's it?" I asked him after translating for Declan. "If you get access to the port, we can count on peace between you and the Bora?"

"That's it," Yoni agreed. He had a joyless smile. In the middle of it was a gold incisor that matched the inlay of the tiles.

Declan and I sighed with relief.

"Tell him he's a fine man and I hope he gets elected mayor," Declan told me. We both shook Yoni's hand.

It was as we headed to the door that Yoni had his afterthought.

"Oh, yes," he added. "And the Nanay, of course."

We stopped at the edge of the courtyard.

"Perdóneme?"

"The Nanay," Yoni clarified. "We would like access to the Rio Nanay for our eco-tours once we get them started. It is one of the *más puro* regions near Iquitos so we would like to take our tourists there."

"The Río Nanay is Iquito country," I pointed out to the man.

Yoni nodded. *"Sí."*

"The Iquito don't want tourists there. They want to be left alone."

Yoni shrugged.

Declan and I returned to our seats. Declan sat for a long time without saying anything. He simply stared at Yoni, trying to figure him out. Yoni sat quietly, too, his eyes wide, his expression blank, like an owl who has been asked to justify eating a mouse.

"Señor," Declan began, "there are other rivers."

"Not like the Nanay."

"It's the Amazon jungle. There are plenty of pristine areas."

"Not like the Nanay."

"The Iquito want to protect their culture. Tourist boats going by every day will destroy it."

Yoni shrugged.

"What else is up the Nanay River that you want?" Declan asked point-blank. "There's more to what you want than eco-tours. What else is on the Nanay?"

The owl merely blinked.

Later, as Declan and I walked back to the hotel, he commented, "Do you remember what Juan said the other day about Oten? When he was trying to explain why Oten – a Witato who should know better – had agreed with the loggers to cut down the forest, Juan said 'Oten had moved to town.' I thought he was just saying that Oten lived in town, but now I realize he was talking about Oten's character. Well, this guy Yoni has gone to town, too."

"I agree," I said. "Let's hope he doesn't get elected mayor."

***

That night the three of us walked over to Jaime's for dinner. The Malecón was dark. To the east only a sliver of moon hung near the horizon and the rays it skipped across the surface of the Amazon barely touched the bluffs below the city. In the same quadrant of sky thunderstorms were forming. There was enough moonlight to see them build, their clouds turning hostile against the pinprick stars. When lightning flickered we could make out the rain shafts hanging below, standing weakly under their load as though at any moment the cap above would grow too large and cause the whole structure to topple onto the jungle.

"Buenas noches," Jaime greeted us at the door. As always he wore a linen shirt over loose pants, the picture of relaxation. He looked like a plantation owner who had just roused himself from the library where he had been sipping rum and perusing a history of the sugar trade.

"Hello, Jaime. Thanks for setting up our meeting with the Bora."

He held a cigar to his lips and puffed.

"Well, of all the grave robbers who come to my restaurant, you are the best-dressed," he exhaled, "so it is only right that I do my small part to assist you." He blew rings toward the sky and regarded me with heavy eyes. "Really, you Americans have too much time on your hands."

"You don't know the half of it," I told him.

Inside, the Bora waited.

Big Jane wasn't quite Jabba the Hut as people had described her to us. When we walked in she was already seated in a corner of Jaime's place, flanked by members of her clan. But while it was hard to guess her height, there was no doubt about her girth. Broad in the face, her figure expanded from there on down. She was at least as wide as the two men perched to her left and right. Her chest merged into her stomach, which bulged before her so much her fleshy arms barely reached the table behind which her group sat. She occupied the room the way Buddha occupies a temple. I wondered what kind of chair was holding her up.

We had been briefed that she was a little coarse. As if to confirm it, as we entered the building she put down a bottle of beer and belched loudly. There was a strong smell of sweat and unwashed bodies.

Declan tapped Tommy on the arm. "She's all yours," he said.

"Buenas," I greeted the Bora.

"Uds. quieren algo," was her reply. "You want something. You want something from the Bora. What is it?"

"Ah," said Tommy, "a woman who is direct." Ignoring the fumes, he swung a chair around and plopped himself down across from her. "I like that!"

She glared at him. "Who are you?"

"I'm Tommy!" he declared with a big smile.

"Are you someone special?"

"You know it, *señora*. Every woman since my mother has said so."

Big Jane groaned aloud. "Jaime!" she barked. "Your restaurants have always had insects but now some of them are coming through the door. Must I put up with this?"

Jaime seated himself. With a wave of his cigar like a conductor prepping his orchestra, he motioned for his waitress to bring everyone a round of drinks. The action calmed Jane and gave the rest of us time to find our own places around the table.

"Perhaps I will get another restaurant," Jaime sighed in his late-night-radio voice. "And it will have big doors and little doors and all sizes in between so that insects and elephants and all manner of God's creatures can come to my table. The conversation then will be exquisite."

To my ears he had just called Bora Jan an elephant.

"No," she said. "Then your restaurant will just be loud. Let's get down to business."

I looked at Declan. "The dream speech?" I muttered.

"Don't waste your time," he whispered back. "Don't mention the skull, either. Make something up about why we're involved, then emphasize how the Bora will benefit by playing ball. This broad doesn't care about dreams."

The group of men with Big Jane didn't matter. She never introduced them. I think they were just there to pick her up in case the chair broke.

She dominated the conversation anyway. Jaime insisted on some small talk but quickly the conversation turned to what we were trying to do and how the Bora were involved. Despite Declan's admonition, I went ahead and presented Walt's dream as the reason for our presence. I had to for otherwise I couldn't come up with a remotely plausible reason why we cared about the commercial arrangements of the tribes without wanting a cut ourselves. But I did steer away from the skulls. In broad terms I sketched how we wanted the Bora to patch things up with the Witoto, and further how it would benefit them to work alongside the Yaguar at the Iquitos port. I stressed the potential that Iquitos held as a tourist destination and how the Bora were in a prime position to profit from the increased traffic. Never once did I mention skulls.

Big Jane listened as I talked, her face registering greater contempt the further I got in my story. She wasn't an ugly woman. For all her size, her face had features that suggested that as a child she had been cute and pudgy. But now it was hard to appreciate those features with all the flab around them. Not to mention the scowl that she twisted it into.

When I finished, she took a long pull of her Cuzqueña and belched again.

"*Pendejado,*" she announced. I had been in Peru long enough to know that was their word for bullshit.

"Pardon?"

She scowled at each one of us in turn. "*No me vengas con sandeces.* That story is complete bullshit."

Jaime propped his feet on an adjacent table and blew smoke rings toward the ceiling. That was his way of saying that we were on our own.

"*Es verdad,*" I insisted.

"*No, no es verdad,*" she mocked me. "*Es pendejado.*"

We argued back and forth to no effect. I was about to give up when Tommy interrupted.

"Baby, it's the truth," he assured her. "Relax. Look at me. Look at this face – is this a face that would lie to you?"

Big Jane looked at him like he was stoned. "Who *are* you?" she demanded again.

"I'm Tommy!" he repeated with his patented grin.

"Tommy who?"

"Just Tommy."

"And why are you calling me *bebe*?" she demanded.

"Because you are one big baby," he oozed in a line that I was sure would result in her reaching across the table and pulling his head right off his neck. Even Jaime tensed for an explosion.

But instead of exploding, Big Jane hesitated, her eyebrows twisted in confusion. Tommy's statement was so ludicrous even she didn't know how to react. But she recovered and fell back on her favorite word, finding delight in being crude.

"*Bueno*, Tommy," she derided him. "You are *pendejado*. You are full of bullshit!"

He laughed. "*Sí, señora!* Of course I am full of bullshit! I am a man! Have you ever met a man who was *not* full of bullshit?"

Now it was Big Jane's turn to laugh. "No!" she snapped back. "I have not. And since we have now established that all of you are full of bullshit, stop wasting my time and tell me what you are doing here – and don't give me any more crap about some dream," she snarled, looking straight at me.

I sat back, defeated. Since Tommy had the wind at his back I motioned that the negotiations were now his. He accepted, slid another beer across to Big Jane, and gave her a wink.

"Alright, *señora*," he said. "Here's the deal." He went over my story again in detail, this time including our interest in the skulls and how our negotiations with the Iquito and the Witato tied in with what we wanted the Bora to do. Several times Jane interrupted him but each time Tommy cut her off by slapping the table and yelling, "Damn it, woman! Let me finish or I'll smack your big ass!" She giggled each time he did – but she let him continue. Then when he ended his tale she actually thought for a minute before responding.

"That cannot be bullshit," she decided. "Nobody would invent a story that stupid." Tommy took that as a compliment. She glared at him. "And the Yaguar?" she asked, her eyes narrowing. "What demands do they make of the Bora?"

Tommy motioned to Declan, who spoke while Tommy translated. Big Jane listened impatiently. When he dwelled on the benefits of the Bora opening up the docks she waved her hand to get him to come to his point. When he described the Yaguar plan for eco-tours she stopped him.

"The Yaguar do not want *ecoturismo*," she lectured us, her tone indicating how naive she thought we were.

"*Bueno, señora,*" I said. "I believe they do. That is what everyone we have talked to has told us."

"Well, I am telling you they do not," she snapped. Like a teacher with a slow student, she took on an elaborately patient tone. "The Yaguar cannot run even a simple business," she explained. "If they sold ice cream in the Plaza de Armas and tried to give it away, they would fail. Why would they want to try something that involves boats, and advertising, and dealing with *extranjeros*? Did any of you men who are full of bullshit ask yourselves that question?"

I translated for Declan and he nodded. "Actually, yes," he muttered. "I've been wondering the same thing ever since we spoke to Yoni."

Big Jane scowled. "Who of the Yaguar do you talk to?" she demanded.

I told her about Judge Yoni. Then for the first time she turned and spoke rapidly to her companions in their own language. Whatever they said, they came to agreement quickly.

"Whatever Yoni told you, he lied," she informed us. "Let me tell you something of the Yaguar. They are lazy and always take the short cut. Especially that man. If he told you something, it is not true. He is not even a good Yaguar. He cares only for himself."

From that point the discussion bogged down. With the Yaguar proposal established as unreliable – at least in Big Jane's eyes – negotiations on the other issues stopped. The only good thing that came out of the evening was that this branch of the Bora was also willing to bargain with the Witato. That, and neither Jane nor her companions posed any fresh demands. Declan and I went home around eleven o'clock, pondering our next step. When we left, Tommy and Big Jane were still at the table, drinking and happily shouting insults at each other. Jaime lounged nearby, blowing smoke rings and likely wondering if he shouldn't move his restaurant again, this time to a more private location.

***

Work intervened over the next several days. We flew more gas out to Site 7 and to a new LZ near the Huallaga River. Since our loadmaster, Harley Fisher, came down with food poisoning all three of us pilots had to go along on those trips. Once the missions were over, though, Declan returned to his diplomatic efforts in earnest, shuttling between the four tribes as much as Henry Kissinger ever attacked the Middle East.

"That big bitch was right," he told us over dinner one night. "Judge Yoni is the sticking point."

"How so?"

"He's got something up his sleeve about the Nanay River. I think it might be logging again. He refuses to compromise even the slightest bit and keeps insisting it has to do with eco-tourism. But I had a kid take me to some Yaguar stores and you know what? Big Jane has them pegged: the Yaguar wouldn't succeed at that any better than they do anything else. They would have to outsource it. And I think the rest of the Yaguar know it. There's another judge, a junior guy, who seems to me more sincere than Yoni. He's willing to compromise but he can't override his boss. However their culture works, Yoni is the decision-maker even if no one else in the community agrees. Pompous old bird."

"Want me to have Big Jane sit on him?" Tommy offered. "She doesn't like the guy any more than you do. He's the one who instigates most of the legal complaints against the Bora and keeps the two communities at each other's throats. For all their talk, the Bora don't fight, but in this case she might be willing to make an exception."

"You know, it's funny," Declan reflected. "The way Juan talked about her, I thought she would be the biggest obstacle for us – excuse the pun. But you've converted her big time, Tommy: every time I talk to her she's like, 'Well, what does that arrogant bastard Tommy say? If it's alright with him, it's alright with us.' I hope you didn't have to sleep with her to win her over." He shivered. "The thought gives me the willies."

Tommy laughed. "You have to look past all that and see her inner beauty, you skinny, shallow man."

Declan belched loudly in reply. "Like that?"

"Exactly!"

***

With a week left, Declan was still pounding his head against the wall. He couldn't find a way to close the loop on the various conflicts without the cooperation of the Yaguar. The Iquito were willing to hunt upriver and cede the northern lands to the Witato. They would also return Oten's head and those of his companions. In return, the Witato would stay out of Iquito territory and hunt the adjacent land sparingly – but only if they could make up for it through fishing in the Momón. The Bora would allow the Witato to fish but needed to make up for their lost territory through activity in town, activity which kept being impeded by the Yaguar. And the Yaguar wanted – well, we knew what they wanted and that was a non-starter. On a trip back to the Iquito with Juan, Declan had raised the topic of eco-tours with Tibau Oma and the reaction was explosive. Declan returned and said he would never go back, he had been so afraid of being killed. Even Juan admitted that the moment had been touch-and-go.

"I don't know what to do," Declan said one evening, rubbing his face in his hands. We sat in the Plaza de Armas across from Ari's Burger, letting Tonio and another boy shine our sneakers. After the sun went down but before it grew dark, the air in Iquitos turned gray for half an hour as the day worked itself through the transition. Colors dimmed and the pavement and dust seemed to rise into the air to make everything one shade. "I've tried everything with that guy but he won't budge. He's going to sink this deal. Damn. I'm usually pretty good at stuff like this."

The boy brushing Declan's shoes was the nine-year-old translator he had taken with him upriver. The boy was trying to learn English better so he listened carefully to our conversation. His English was good but he had spent too much time with the Navy SEALs – everything was fuck this and fuck that.

"Who is it that gives you trouble?" he asked.

"What? Nothing. Just a judge who is trying to get something for himself and we don't want him to have it."

"What judge?"

"Why?" I smiled. "Do you know many judges?"

"I know everything!" he insisted. It was a street kid mantra.

"Really? Do you know Judge Yoni?"

The boy didn't. He asked Tonio, who punched him in the shoulder and pointed out that he did in fact know Yoni. Tonio described the judge, pointed off toward Loreto Plaza, and finished by tapping one of his incisors. The younger boy said, "Ahhh," and changed his answer.

"*Sí*, I know him. He comes to the fucking docks."

"Yes, he wants a boat of his own," Declan said. "That's part of our problem."

"He has a boat," the boy said.

"Excuse me?"

"He has a fucking boat," the boy repeated. "He goes out with his friends."

Declan sat up. "What friends? Who are his friends?"

"The fucking Colombians."

We almost fell off the park bench in our surprise. We pumped the kid for information but after a minute of that Tonio interrupted. He was impatient that the conversation was in English and he didn't understand it. Further, he saw that his partner was on to something. He grabbed the smaller boy, whispered in his ear, and the two pulled off to a distance for a hurried conversation. When they came back, Tonio said, "If you want to know more it is fifty soles."

"Why, you selfish little ankle biter," I told him. "It's his information, not yours."

"We work together."

"I'll bet you do. Alright then, if it's *your* information, then you should give it to us cheap after everything we've done for you."

"Like what?"

"Like what?! You ungrateful brat, how about if we take you back up to Florida and put that rash back on your face? Or have you forgotten that already?"

"No, but that was Vince, not you. If you take me up there, Vince will kill you." He smiled.

He was right about that. Vince *would* kill us if we hurt Tonio. On the other hand, Vince would want a better deal than fifty soles. "If Vince were here you would give him a better price," I pointed out. "Well, we work with Vince so give us a better price."

"Okay, twenty soles."

"That's more like it."

"We don't need any more gouge," Declan interrupted. "Yoni's in with the Colombians. They want to go up the Nanay and cut down trees and he knows the Iquito won't like it. So he's trying to make it a done deal so the tribe has no choice. Boy, he had better hope the Iquito don't find out."

"What are we going to do about it?"

"I don't know," he admitted. "But we should talk to Jaime and get his opinion. And we had better do it fast."

Tonio whined and moaned about not getting his bribe. When we left the Plaza he had his cohort by the ear and was giving him hell.

***

We didn't see Jaime until the following afternoon when we met him in his front garden for Pisco sours. He heard our story and sat in silence for a while, nodding at the logic of it all. But when he spoke it was to voice disagreement.

"It makes sense," he said. "*Eco-turismo* would be more work than Yaguar are willing to do, so it is not a surprise that he has talked to Colombians. But I do not think it is logging they are interested in."

"Why not?"

"That, too, is work. It is also not easy to hide. I would think that after their last experience the Colombians would want something that is a lower profile."

A lower profile? What else could you do on a river that was... As soon as I pondered the question I knew the answer. A vision came into my mind of the barges in Venezuela that plied the back-country, movable strip mines that sucked up the river bottom in search of gold.

"Mining," I said. "He wants to mine the Nanay! Someone must have gone up there and determined there are minerals worth taking, so now Yoni wants to be part of it."

Jaime unwrapped an El Credito. He did it like he did everything else, carefully, as though there were hidden messages in each motion and he didn't want to miss one by moving too fast. He lit the cigar and puffed to get it going. Then he sat back and looked past its embers, out across the floating city of Belén to where the Amazon flowed beneath a pink sky.

"It could be," he agreed. "But if so, he had better hope the Iquito do not find out."

***

With five days remaining before our return to Panama, Tommy, Declan, and I discussed our options. Tommy wanted to tell the Bora what Yoni was planning to do. I wanted to confront Yoni directly. I thought that if we told Yoni what we knew and threatened to expose the plan, he would give it up and be willing to work with us. Declan, a better read of people, figured that just the opposite would happen. If we threatened Yoni, he argued, he would either ignore us and proceed with mining anyway, or he would shrug, cancel the project, and then cause just as many problems for the Bora as always.

In the end we decided to do both.

Tommy went to see Big Jane. She heard him out, cursed a blue streak, and then admitted that the Bora had once considered aqua-mining, too. They had decided against it once they realized that it could wipe out the fishing industry for miles around. Fishing was in the Bora blood. But as for Yoni, she wasn't sure what leverage any of them had. "He had just better hope the Iquito don't find out," she warned.

Declan agreed to go see Yoni but first he made the rounds of his other contacts to get his ducks in a row. He went back upriver to see Otto, and to see the stinky Bora at the shipwreck, and back to Bora Jan, and even to the junior Yaguar judge, pleading with all of them to make a deal so that everyone could move forward if we could just bring Yoni on board. He went everywhere except back to the Iquito.

All heard him out. Declan – even speaking through his nine-year-old – had gotten quite passionate on the subject. He was to the point where agreement had nearly become its own end. He had almost forgotten about Walt's skull. Almost. He was certain that one of Oten's party was the subject of Walt's vision and that this was his last, best chance to lay hands on it. But even if he had forgotten, the tribes hadn't. By now everyone had heard the complete story of our interest – the Bora, the Yaguar, and certainly the Witato knew what we wanted and assumed that was the real reason for Declan's zeal. But they listened to him anyway. Listened...and told him that it all depended on Yoni.

Finally, at mid-week Declan and I walked down to the Loreto Plaza. Yoni's office was deserted and he was nowhere around. We asked Tonio to track him down but Tonio, remarkably, came up empty. We couldn't find Tonio's little friend at the docks to ask him, either. Old Feo said he had seen Yoni go out on a boat and that the nine-year-old had gone with him, but couldn't tell us where they had gone. When was that? Yesterday, Old Feo said. Or maybe the day before. So just when we wanted him most, our judge vanished.

Tommy and Declan flew out to Site 8 the next day. Declan had to think of something else for a while so we convinced him to take the sortie. I hung around in town but nothing happened to reward my vigil.

***

We were due to leave on Saturday. Friday Declan raced around trying to see his various contacts for one last-ditch effort to forge a compromise. After Yoni's disappearance, though, his shuttle diplomacy broke down. Without Yoni, Declan had no deal. Without a deal, he had nothing to offer. Now nobody would see him. Tommy got in to see Big Jane but she told him that the tribes had decided to handle their relations without outside help. They were talking now and whatever solution they came to would be their own. Thanks but no thanks, was how Tommy interpreted her attitude. But she got drunk with him anyway.

The Yaguar junior judge, Yucay, sent a message to Declan requesting a meeting. That got him excited but when he showed up at the judge's place there was another message saying Yucay had had to cancel. We tried to find him but Tonio, too, had disappeared. We saw the nine-year-old in the Plaza de Armas but lost him in the crowds before we could talk to him. Just when we were under the most pressure to get things done, we felt isolated.

We ate dinner that night at the Pollo Suave on 28 July Plaza. Big Jane had recommended it so we felt obligated to go. Walking back to our hotel we spied Juan Maldonado corralling customers over at Ari's and cut over to see him. He, too, had been gone for a few days but in his case we knew where. His trips up to the Momón with Declan reminded him how much he enjoyed being in the jungle so he was spending more time with Otto and Oten's family. He mentioned that they were now thinking of running ecotours themselves. He also had bad news.

"The Witato have reached an agreement with the Iquito," he told us. "The Iquito will return Oten's skull. You convinced them they can move forward. But the Witato will not let you have the heads for your dream."

"What?!" Declan couldn't believe it. "I thought we had an understanding!"

Juan shrugged. His flies had given up circling for the day and now clung to his hat, resting.

"Otto never really liked the idea," he reminded us. "He convinced the others. They will reach an agreement with the Bora without your help so they have decided to reunite the heads of the victims with their bodies. That is the right thing, yes?"

Of course it was. I felt bad for Declan but at the same time was relieved. After everything Oten and his partners had been through, the least anyone could do was let them rest in peace.

But Declan was crushed. One glimmer of hope after another over the last three weeks had let him believe that getting Oten's skull was foreordained. Even now he hoped that if he found Yoni there was still time to bargain. But if the Witato and Iquito were talking, the game was up. He had failed.

A street urchin we didn't know appeared and told us that Jaime wanted to see us. Declan was depressed and refused to go so Tommy and I walked over to the Malecón by ourselves. We sat inside Jaime's place as a light rain fell, munching yucca frita and drinking beer. Jaime offered us cigars. We sat talking of the world until out of the blue he commented, "Yoni is dead. His boat sank. In the Nanay."

It was so unexpected that we didn't answer. A bat whipped by our table and flew up to a spot on the ceiling above the beams. It was only one so nobody got excited, but Jaime frowned and pointed it out to the waitress, who went for a ladder.

Tommy found his tongue. "In the Nanay. That's a hell of a coincidence."

Jaime didn't agree or disagree. In any conversation most of his words were directed to his cigar and this one was no different. He contemplated the ash as he spoke. "It was the Iquito who found the boat. It happened Monday or Tuesday so the piranha have had days to work. The Iquito say there is nothing left of him or his companions."

"How do you know all this?" I asked. "This is the first we've heard of it."

It was a stupid question so Jaime didn't bother to answer. Asking anyone down south how or where they got their information was bad form and I sometimes forgot that.

"Yucay will make decisions now," Jaime added.

That's a good thing, I thought, before remembering that Declan wouldn't get his skulls regardless of who made decisions for the Yaguar, so who really cared? Yes, in the big picture the tribes might have turned a corner in their relations but what did that do for Walt's dream? Not a thing.

Back at the El Dorado, Tommy and I woke Declan to tell him the news. From the pillow he muttered, "The Bora did it."

"Huh?"

"The Bora. They sink boats."

He was a true cynic. I had taken Jaime's story at its face value: boats in Peru ran about as well as the *motocarros* did – they broke down all the time so believing that one had sunk on its own was easy for me. Granted, it was a bit convenient that Yoni's had gone down in the Nanay but since that's where we thought he was thinking of mining it still made sense.

Tommy was more like Declan, except partial to the Bora. He assumed Yucay had engineered the overthrow of his boss.

"What about the Witato?" I suggested. "They had as much motive as anybody. Except for the Iquito, of course."

"The Iquito don't come into town," Tommy reminded me. "They would have needed help."

When he said that, the three of us looked at each other.

"They would have needed help," Declan repeated.

"They all had motive," Tommy added.

I thought of Tonio's friend, the kid at the docks. "Old Feo said he went out on the boat with Yoni," I reminded them. "But we saw him this afternoon."

"So he came back somehow. But if the boat sank, how did he get back?" Declan wanted to know. "Unless..."

"Unless someone brought him back."

"And if someone brought him back..."

"Then maybe it wasn't an accident."

Declan was wide awake now. As we discussed the situation, Tommy tried to find humor in it, joking that we had succeeded in fostering inter-tribal cooperation better than we had hoped. But Declan and I were worried. I wondered if there wasn't an angle we were missing, one that put us in danger as well.

"We need to leave," I concluded.

"You're right about that," Declan agreed. "I don't know what you guys normally do down here, but if it's anything like this I'm going to stick to Honduras from now on."

***

The next morning we were out at the airport and ready for take-off by ten o'clock. We would have left earlier but on weekends in Iquitos it was impossible to get the tower to open the airfield before all the controllers had recovered from their hangovers the night before. Tommy had the APU going and Declan was running pre-flight checklists when Harley waved to us from outside.

"Tonio's here," he said over the intercom.

We looked out the window. Harley was out front ready to monitor the start but he pointed to the edge of the apron where Tonio stood beside an idling *motocarro*. He carried a cardboard take-out box from the Pollo Suave.

"What's he got?"

Harley went over and had a conversation with Tonio but when he reached for the box Tonio pulled it away. He pointed toward Declan who he could see through the open cockpit window.

"He says it's for you, L-T. Must be lunch."

"Me?" asked Declan.

"Yeah. Special delivery. Can't trust no stinking loadmaster with it." Harley walked back to his post.

Declan turned to me. "Mike, go get it, will you?"

"Gotcha."

Declan shouted to Tonio to give me the box. Tonio wouldn't approach the C-27, though, so I walked to the grass to meet him.

"You want to see the plane?" I asked.

"No." He held a hand over one ear to block out the noise from the APU.

"It's pretty cool inside."

"No!"

"Okay, okay. I'll take the box."

"Twenty soles."

"What? Why, what is it?"

Tonio shrugged.

"Where did you get it?"

"Juan Maldonado."

"Alright, then."

I gave him his money and he handed over the box. Declan's name was written in block scrawl across the top.

"Is there any trouble back in town?" I asked as he turned to go.

Tonio hopped onto the *motocarro* as the driver revved the engine.

"Why would there be?" he asked. They sped off.

I jumped back into the cabin and handed the box up to Declan. "Tonio's getting an attitude."

"Getting? He's had one. What is it?"

"Something from Juan. Maybe it's lunch."

"I thought it might have been for me," Tommy whined as Declan whipped out his knife and cut the string on the box. "From Big Jane. A going away present to her main man."

"You ought to be grateful she hasn't come out here herself wanting to go with you. In another week you might have had to marry her."

"Fat women need love, too," he pointed out. "But you're right. Let's go before she shows up."

Declan opened the box. Then with no warning he yelled, "Aurhgh!!" and threw it off his lap. It hit the overhead panel but I caught it before it landed on the floor.

"What the..." I said, and peered inside. "Aurhgh!!!" I whipped around and threw the box into the cabin, then clambered up into the cockpit to get away from it. Declan was already climbing out his side window.

"Is it alive?" Tommy yelled. "Load, get a gun!"

But the box wasn't alive. It hit the floor of the cabin and upended, throwing out some rags and letting the ball inside roll halfway to the ramp. Except it wasn't a ball. It was a skull, round in the face and recently occupied, picked clean the way only a thousand fish can and bleached as white as a fresh boiling could make it. One gold tooth shone smack in the center of its joyless smile.

Declan was out on the tarmac, puking up his breakfast. I, too, jumped outside for the benefit of fresh air and distance. Only Tommy stayed in his seat, speechless.

Harley charged aboard with his 9mm but put it away when he saw the cause of the commotion. Loadmasters are impossible to gross out so he nudged the skull with his toe. "Anybody we know?" he asked.

"Local politician," I explained, looking in from the ramp.

"The guy you couldn't find? Well, you found him."

There was a piece of paper on the floor next to the rags. Harley glanced at it and handed it to me. It read, BUEN SUERTE CON TU VISION. Y GRACIAS. JUAN

Declan peeked in through the door.

"Wrap it up, will you, Load?" he said weakly.

"You want to take it with us?"

Declan waved away all questions. "We need to get out of here," he said. Crawling into the cabin, he added, "Guess we don't have to worry about him being mayor."

***

In Panama we stayed mum about the trip except for quietly letting Walt know that we were quite certain we had his skull. Walt caught our drift and advised us to sit on it for a few weeks. Tommy kept it, which was the safest thing since nobody would be surprised at anything they found at the Pinheads' house.

But eventually Walt decided that such an important addition to the collection had to be unveiled. Our tradition up to then had been to gather around the ops desk on a Friday afternoon after the leadership had gone home and display for each other anything new that was found for the hunt. We would crack open the beer, relate the circumstances of the discovery, and recognize who had done the finding. So a month or so after we returned from Iquitos it was the skull's turn.

"This one was difficult," Walt addressed the crowd.

"As opposed to the box of bird crap that Lowell dug up?" Charlie Manson asked from the back of the room. He thought the hunt was stupid but enjoyed hearing what the rest of us went through as part of it.

"No, no," said Walt. "That was hard, too, and we all appreciate Lowell's efforts. And I assume his wounds have healed."

Lowell muttered under his breath.

"No, this one was uniquely challenging," Walt continued. "Lots of people including me looked for this particular item but we all came up short. It was only Declan, with help from Tommy and Mike, who had a sense of what was needed and how to make it happen. So without further ado, I want to show what they were able to find..."

The door to the hangar slammed open. Little Bud stormed in, followed by two OSI agents and Major Farnham. He pointed to the box on the ops counter and thundered, "There's been a murder! These people are all in on a cover-up and the evidence is RIGHT THERE."

The OSI agents looked uncertain. Major Farnham was apologetic. "Uh, Captain Manson, what's going on here?" he asked.

Charlie pointed with his beer at Walt. "Don't look at me, sir. He's in charge."

Walt displayed cherubic innocence. "Hey, sir. Would you like a beer?"

"Don't listen to him, sir," Little Bud warned. "He's the ringleader. They've killed somebody and taken his head, all for some sick mass sacrifice they're involved in. That's it right there, right there on the desk."

Major Farnham accepted a beer from Mike Vaneya. "Thank you. Walt, do you mind showing us what's in the box?"

Walt slid the box across the counter. "By all means, sir. But we were hoping it would be a surprise."

The OSI agents approached the counter and flipped up the box top. Little Bud was close behind. "Have your guns ready. Have your guns ready," he advised them.

They ignored him and peered into the box. Then carefully they reached inside together to lift the object out. It was a dry, cracked, dusty horse's skull. A tiny price tag dangled from the lower jaw.

"Lieutenant Goode got it for you in Peru, sir," Walt explained while Little Bud's own jaw dropped. "We were going to give it to you at your promotion next month."

Farnham stared at the head, confused. Flattered, but confused. "What would I do with it?" he asked.

Tommy shrugged and flashed his everyone-loves-me smile. "Sir, I have no idea. But you would be the only lieutenant-colonel in the wing to have one!"

The major stepped up and examined the gift.

"Sorry about the price tag," Walt said quickly. He reached out and pulled the tag free, which was only there for effect anyway. "Trust me, though. It's priceless."

"Well, uh," Farnham stammered. "I don't know what to say." He took the skull and hefted it. His expression was what one might expect. "Really, what do I do with it?"

"How about a paperweight, sir?" Evan suggested. "If you have that on your desk it'll spark conversation with everyone who sees it."

"I should say so."

"A round of applause," Charlie suggested, and we all clapped. That made Farnham feel good. Any doubts faded away.

"Alright, gentlemen. I've never received a stranger gift but for just that reason I'll accept it." He frowned. "I'm going to need a bigger desk..."

Little Bud didn't know what to do. He pulled the box off the counter and peered inside.

"Sir, this isn't what I wanted you to see. I believe..."

"Lieutenant Blair," Major Farnham interrupted him. "You're a strange one. You could have made up a simpler story to get me over here but I guess this worked, so thank you."

"But sir, I..."

"And you men must have been in on it, too," he added to the OSI agents, who were beginning to think they were being made fun of. "Thank you." One of the agents checked his watch and glowered at Little Bud. They soon slipped out of the room.

"Now, let's drink some beer!" Major Farnham announced. "It's on me!"

At some point I sidled over to Walt. "Where's the real skull?" I asked.

"We were getting to that," he replied. Behind him Tommy lounged in a chair with his feet propped on a box marked Printer Supplies. "But there was no way we could meet without Little Bud getting wind of it so we thought we would help him out."

"By making him look like a jackass?"

"He's the easiest set-up in the world. Look at him, pouting like somebody ran over his dog. You would think he would be grateful. Without us he would have nothing to do on Friday afternoon."

"You think he'll stop spying now?" I asked.

Walt studied his beer. "I hope not. Kurt's going to introduce him to a girl from the Russian consulate next week. If we work it right, we may see him transfer to Moscow before the end of the year."

4

Maximón

There were actually twenty-seven items on Walt's list. We thought for the longest time there were only twenty-six but one day at a hail-and-farewell Walt admitted he had been holding out.

"There's a guy," he said.

"What do you mean, a guy?"

We stood around the apron outside the hangar. It was a Friday, one of those afternoons where everyone decided that if the task they were working on wasn't done by two o'clock it probably wasn't worth doing. People drifted outside in anticipation of the four o'clock sendoff for a couple of C-130 guys who were transferring back to the States. Walt already had a beer in him so when Josh did what he always did and started pointing out the absurdity of the treasure hunt, Walt decided to make Josh's point for him.

"There was one other thing that popped up in the dream," he explained. "You guys already thought I was crazy so I didn't mention it at the time. It's a guy."

"A homo type guy?" Lowell scowled, determined that the answer be yes.

"No, not that I know of," Walt said patiently. "But weird. I'm not sure how to describe him."

"This isn't the old pilot?" I asked. "It's someone else?"

"Definitely somebody else. This one came from up north."

"What did he look like?"

Walt chuckled, knowing we wouldn't believe him.

"Picture Adolphe Menjou gone bad."

"Huh?"

He stared across the runway to where the control tower poked out of the jungle. "Okay, picture a Mexican thug except well-dressed. Well, not well-dressed but like he *was* well-dressed and then raided a gypsy's wardrobe and threw a bunch of that stuff over his suit. A jacket and tie but then a red cape and a blue sash around his waist. Long hair. Black hair. Maybe a pony tail. And a hat. A black hat, could be a Homburg. Dark sunglasses. Definitely dark sunglasses with a huge moustache, dark skin, and a cigar. Can you picture that?"

Josh burst out laughing. "I can picture you being grounded and sent to Mental Health for evaluation!" he replied.

"Like the rest of it makes sense?"

"Walt, are you serious? This guy appeared in your dream?"

"Yes, he did. But it wasn't like he walked up and talked to me. I mean, all those hands were holding things up and the next thing I know this guy pops out of Central America and is standing there in mid-air. I think he was standing there. He may have been sitting... All of a sudden he's just there, staring at me. Dressed like I said."

Josh stared at him. "You're the weirdest person I know," he told Walt. "I used to think it was Big Bud but now it's you."

"Thank you," Big Bud said. He was standing behind Lowell and until he spoke none of us knew he was there.

"Weird or not, Mexican Guy is out there," Walt replied. "And I'm damned if I know what we have to do to find him."

"If he's in Mexico, we won't," Rolo stated flatly. "We don't fly there."

"I didn't say he was in Mexico," Walt clarified. "I just said he looked like a Mexican gangster. He could be anywhere."

I thought back on the last half-dozen Panamanian cops who had written me tickets. Most of them looked like Tijuana mobsters. Mexican Guy could indeed be anywhere.

Lt Col Rasmussen came out of the hangar just then with Maj Farnham and the C-130 crew. We put the beer down and got ready to listen to speeches.

"Nothing personal," Josh whispered to Walt, "but you're as nutty as they come. If you ever run across that Mexican guy, I suggest you run away as fast as you can."

***

But when it came to nutty Josh pushed the envelope himself. He showed up at the ops desk one day wearing a yarmulke. That wasn't crazy by itself – there were plenty of Jewish people in the military who wore skullcaps and their wear was even included in the uniform regulations. But on Josh – Mr Party Hard, live-for-today, sleep with as many women as possible before they find out what a scumbag you are – it was downright ludicrous. Him wearing a yarmulke was as religious as Hugh Hefner wearing a mitre. The wear of a religious garment implies piety and self-discipline. Josh thought piety was a small dessert.

But one day he appeared with a yarmulke nonetheless, not saying a word. When people stared at him he stared back, daring them to comment. They did, of course, and when they did he got defensive.

Within hours of slapping it on he had argued with almost everyone in the squadron. But that was his fault. He should have expected the scrutiny. Our squadron was all men and Rule #1 for men is to make fun of your friends as often as you can. Josh learned quickly that if he was going to wear a beanie, we were all going to help him do it.

"Still toying with religion, I see," I commented when I saw him. "Carrying your interest to the next level?"

He held up a hand to ward off further input.

"You can save your comments," he informed me. "The Pinheads were already in here. Before them was Lowell. And before him was the loadmaster mafia. They came down because Charlie Manson told them they had to see it for themselves."

"Charlie had a crack at you, too?"

"First thing, which isn't fair because nobody should have to deal with Charlie first thing in the morning. He's not even original – 'what the hell is that? Breakfast get out of hand and a pancake land on your head?' That's supposed to be funny?"

I logged into the scheduling computer, then sat back and watched him pretend to concentrate on updating the sorties on the grease board. The yarmulke perfectly covered his bald spot but the hairpins holding it weren't level so it bubbled up on one side like a poorly-ironed doily.

"Is it supposed to lie like that?"

"Oh, come on, Mike! Don't you start with me, too."

"I'm just asking. It's a fair question – you're not exactly the pious type, Josh."

He threw down the markers he used to list the sorties – blue for local lines, red for last-minute changes, green for overnights somewhere in the jungle – and collapsed into a chair. He fumbled with the yarmulke, finally pulling it off and plopping it into his lap where he adjusted the pins.

"Alright," he said quietly. "You're right. I'm not exactly Rabbi Small. I just thought I'd try it out, you know? I've been going to synagogue and..."

"Synagogue?" I repeated. "You've been going *to synagogue*? You mean to *the* synagogue?"

"No, I mean *to synagogue*. That's the way we say it, just like you Catholics say *going to church* instead of going to *the* church."

"Yeah, but I've at least been to church in my lifetime. You talk as though you're re-born."

He played with the pins. Already the border of the yarmulke had begun to fray.

"Oh, you've got to be kidding me," he exclaimed. "Look at this! I paid $12 for it and it's already falling apart! They're replacing this. Even if I threw out the receipt they're replacing this. This is junk..."

Evan came in from the hangar and wandered past the desk, eyeing Josh's scalp as he did. Josh glared back and Evan wisely kept his silence until departing out the other door.

"I was just trying it out," Josh repeated when Evan was gone. The look in his eyes asked me to understand. "I went to the synagogue but it didn't feel right – the rabbi's a nice guy and he knows a lot of stuff but I just felt out of place. Then I thought, maybe if I try to dress the part a little more, you know, it might be easier to fit in. I'm not religious but you can become religious, right? Maybe if I try...if I go through the motions for a while and make an honest effort, maybe it'll work out. It could be like walking into cold water where if you just do a little at a time eventually you stop thinking about it and before you know it you're swimming. Maybe then it'll make sense." For a moment he grew eager, pondering his own metaphor. Then he laughed, folded the yarmulke gently, and slipped it into his pocket. "And maybe not."

I liked Josh more when he was less complicated. Still, he was my friend. I motioned toward his hairline.

"Wear whatever you want, dude. If it works for you then forget everybody else."

"You think?"

"Of course."

He thought for a moment but then shook his head.

"Nah. They're right."

"Well, whatever you do, don't become a Griswold Beckett, okay?" I pleaded, referring to our resident religious fanatic who was also a bad pilot. "Please? For all our sakes, remember how to take off and land."

"I will," he sighed. "Don't worry."

***

For months we heard no more of Josh's midlife crisis. He went back to being the guy we all knew and loved – or at least the guy we all knew and could count on to be shallow and self-centered. He stopped talking to the rabbi and stopped visiting the synagogue. Conversations reverted to money and flying. He joined Amway and became the squadron pill peddling household cleaners and trying to get everyone to sign up to his pyramid scheme.

And of course there were women. While he and I were in Antigua for language school he spent every weekend in Guatemala City, picking up rich girls in clubs and taking them back to the Camino Real to indulge their passion for foreigners. He partied so much that in just a month he managed to get a reputation in club circles as a player –

he bragged that after four weeks he'd slept with so many girls the only reason any of the rest still went out with him was to find out what all the fuss was about.

It was in the Camino Real, though, that religion jumped back into his life with both feet. It happened on a Sunday morning, the same day I was flying back to Guatemala City from Tikal after a visit to the ruins. Josh was lying in bed with a university student named Alma who asked him if he would stay loyal to her now that they were together. He assured her that of course he would. How could she be sure, she wanted to know?

"Because I love you," he told her.

"Really?"

"*Absolutamente.* If I'm lying, may God strike me dead."

With that a tremendous explosion shook the building, then reverberated over the city like a thunder clap. The *boom* echoed so long that people looked for a storm in the cloudless sky and then to the rusty walls of the mountains to see if they were falling down.

But the explosion didn't come from a storm or from the mountains. It came from the city airport, known as La Aurora. Unbeknownst to anyone but the Guatemalan military, the nation's army used a hangar on the west side of La Aurora for storing munitions. Piled floor to ceiling inside the hangar was every type of shell in the Guatemalan inventory. Grenades, bullets, mortars, mines – every conceivable make of explosive including open bags of gunpowder sat on shelves in a drafty fifty-year-old hangar with conscript soldiers to guard them. They were exposed to damp, rust, heat, and the rumble of aircraft and street traffic, not to mention any undisciplined recruit smoking a cigarette. That Sunday the hangar blew up.

The military claimed that Mayan rebels flew over the building and dropped a bomb on it, which was a ludicrous attempt to deflect responsibility that no one believed. Although every bit of evidence was destroyed in the blast – along with a third of the runway, two city streets, and an entire neighborhood of squatters, plus another neighborhood that burned in the resulting fire – the consensus was that either spontaneous combustion or a simple storage accident triggered the detonation.

Over 400 people were killed. Outrage was muted because the victims were poor. In ensuing days the government even claimed the airport was lucky that the hangar was on the far side of the runway and not closer to the terminal where it would have killed more people and destroyed a dozen planes. As it was, black smoke poured across the field for hours, shutting it down and bringing the city to a standstill as every fire department rushed equipment to the scene. Airborne in a local puddle-jumper that was now unable to land, I watched the scene out the window until our pilots finally diverted to Puerto Barrios. Down on the ground, Josh sent his date home and then sat by the window, wondering if God had missed.

"The clock is ticking," he assured me days later as we approached the end of the language course. "That was a sign, Mike. It was a sign that I'm wasting my life in shallow pursuits."

"It was a sign that Guatemalans don't know how to store explosives," I corrected him. "A real sign about your gigolo lifestyle would be if you got syphilis."

"No. I lied to her and then I invoked His name. You can't do that."

"Which? You can't lie or you can't say 'God?'"

"You can't say 'God.' Oh, damn it."

We sat in the bar at the Posada Don Rodrigo, a historic one-story hotel two blocks off the town square. It was our kind of place: quiet, dark, and built of stone and rough wood that had held together for two hundred years and was unlikely to be disturbed by anything we said. Perfect for Josh's brooding. Our month of language training was finished and overall we had both had a great time. But now Josh was beset with guilt. We were ready to leave.

"Who says?"

"The rabbi."

"You're back talking to him again?"

"No, but that's one of the things he told me before. "You can't say G-...you know, that, what you just said. And you can't say the Y-word, or the J-word, or..."

"What are the Y-word and the J-word?" I interrupted.

"Yehova and Jehova. Oh, damn it!" He clapped a hand over his mouth. "You set me up. Why did you do that?"

"Do what? I don't know what you're talking about. You can't say Jehova? Really?"

"It's not funny."

"Can I say them?"

"You can say whatever you want."

"Well, if I can say them why can't you?"

"Because you're not Jewish."

"So?"

"So, God doesn't care what you say. You're going to hell anyway. Oh, *damn* it!"

"Why am I going to hell? I don't sleep around nearly as much as you do."

"But you're not Jewish."

"So?"

"So, you're going to hell."

"Everybody who's not Jewish goes to hell?"

"That's what the conservative guys believe. I figure if I'm going to follow the faith I ought to go with the strictest version of it."

"In my Catholic world everyone goes to heaven," I pointed out. "Not that I believe that, either, but as religions go it's friendlier."

He sniffed. "Catholics...don't get me started. The New Testament is junk. Anyone who believes it is a fool."

"And we're going to hell."

"And you're going to hell." When I tried to reply, he waved his hands to shoo me away. "I don't make the rules, Mike."

"But you seem to want to follow them."

"Yeah. No. Oh, hell. I don't even know most of them," he admitted, rubbing his face in his hands. "And maybe following them is just as pointless as what I'm doing now. But it might be time for me to give it a try."

***

So even though we didn't hear much about Josh's existential worries they weren't far below the surface. He recovered somewhat after we returned to Panama – the routine of work and being back in his own apartment with its modern conveniences and luxurious bar helped to mellow his mood and remind him that cultural evolution had its advantages. He dated a few girls who didn't demand commitment. He made some Amway sales. No lightning bolts struck him on the way to work and his confidence returned. He avoided the synagogue.

But then his dating hit a dry spell and the soap sales stalled. He began to spend nights sitting alone at home reading Barrons and the Old Testament. I knew he was vulnerable. It would take only a small incident – another airport explosion, maybe – to prod his guilt and launch him full-tilt into the religious experience he kept toying with.

***

We were in Panama only a month when the squadron was tapped to send a plane back to La Aurora after an earthquake there knocked out the highway to the north coast. Knowing we were getting another good deal we took a plane back up to Guatemala City to sit alert.

But it turned out that none of the supplies we were supposed to carry ever showed up. The damage to the country's infrastructure proved to be minor and donors changed their minds. So instead of saving lives we spent days sitting around doing nothing. Again talk turned to flying and money. With the former scarce, gaining more of the latter predominated as a topic.

The usual discussions of stocks and real estate lasted for a while. Then on the third day of inactivity Josh had a eureka moment. He was drinking his coffee at breakfast in the stylish restaurant of the Camino Real and happened to read the label on the bag of fresh ground roast. Something clicked. His eyes fell on the suitcase full of cleaning products he had brought up from Panama and so far been unable to sell.

"Mike," he announced. "Let's do a road trip."

We borrowed a pickup and drove over the mountains to Antigua. The region between the volcanoes there was tailor-made for coffee growers: the Arabica beans it produced were prized throughout Latin America. They were also expensive – at least in Panama. A bag bought in Antigua for less than a dollar sold for five times that in the salons of Punta Paitilla. Neither of us had thought to pick up any while at school but now with time on our hands and a suitcase full of domestic wares Josh figured to make a killing through barter with the natives.

"You have toilet brushes," I pointed out to him in confusion, picking through his bags. "Toilet brushes and room fresheners and sponges. Some of these farms won't have toilets, you know. And what's this? Laundry detergent? They won't have washing machines, either. Why would they trade good coffee for Amway junk?"

"Hey, hey, hey! It's not junk. It's domestic necessities. Good household product. Top of the line stuff. And cleaning supplies are universal – brushes, towels, soap. *Premium* powdered soap. Just because it says it's for machines doesn't mean you can't use it in the sink."

"They don't have sinks."

"Zip it."

We drove into the central highlands, into the province of Sacatepéquez, and turned north. A decent road ran through the hills toward Chimaltenango, dipping into beautiful valleys where small farms dotted the landscape and unnamed paths led into the fields. The farms that grew coffee were easy to spot due to their huge shade trees and macadamias interspersed with the crops. We turned into the first of these *fincas* looking for a deal.

"This is good stuff," Josh whispered as he sniffed a burlap bag filled with fresh coffee "cherries." The farmer noted his satisfaction and brought him a smaller bag of semi-processed beans. These gave off an even richer smell. "Yep, yep," Josh nodded happily. "Just what we're looking for! Just what we're looking for!"

The farmer was a thirty-something man who looked like he'd already worked harder that day that we would all week. He was confused but flattered that someone had come specifically to his farm to purchase coffee. Normally he had to take it to town himself to strike the best bargain he could. He watched Josh examine various bags of beans with growing anticipation.

"Hmm..." Josh said eventually, tempering his enthusiasm so he didn't appear anxious. "I don't know..." He wandered through the small barn like a health inspector investigating a tip. Chickens dodged his feet and circled back with cocked heads, wondering what he would decide. But there was no mystery: he wanted the coffee.

Finally he looked out over the five-acre plot and stroked his chin.

"Si!" he announced. "Let's by some coffee! *Vamos a comprar cafe!"*

He turned to the farmer and offered to buy twenty pounds of beans for a dollar a bag. Since that was a twenty percent premium over the going market price the man's eyes almost bugged out of his head.

They went back into their sockets after Josh dragged one of his suitcases out of the truck and explained that he had something better than cash to trade for the coffee.

"Qué es eso?" the man asked me when Josh held up the sponges like they were gold doubloons. I shook my head to indicate that I wasn't part of the barter system. I paid him quetzales for some bags of my own.

"Ah, but quetzales aren't half as useful as these!" Josh insisted, and spent the next ten minutes talking the farmer into a deal that – while on a smaller scale than the purchase of Manhattan – had a lot in common with previous uses of wampum and beads.

"Oh, this was a brilliant idea," he exuded as we drove away with thirty pounds of coffee in the back seat. The bags radiated a heady, caffeinated aroma that carried through the cabin of the minivan. Just hefting one of them gave off a rich scent of dark beans that was invigorating. Josh took extra pleasure knowing that he was getting it at fire-sale prices.

"You don't feel guilty?" I asked.

"What? Why?"

"Well, you just traded about five dollars worth of sponges for fifty dollars worth of coffee. That was some smooth talking you did back there."

"Value is relative. I merely convinced him how useful those sponges could be to him around the farm."

"That you did. When we drove away he looked like he was coming out of a hypnotherapy session."

Josh laughed. "Oh, please. I wasn't that good. But you're right, it was a sweet deal."

"Maybe a little too sweet."

"Oh, now don't you go being all Mister Sensitive Capitalist on me. He's a big boy – he could have said no. And besides, I noticed you weren't so distraught that you didn't buy a few for yourself."

"Yeah, but I paid market price – and in cash."

"Ooo, aren't you special? What difference will that make when you sell all that coffee for a mark-up back in Panama?"

"I'm not going to sell it," I insisted. "These bags are for gifts. I just did half my Christmas shopping."

"Sure you did. And like that makes a difference, anyway. Look, Mr. Morality, if you can't appreciate the market system that's fine, but don't be judging me. I'm giving people stuff they can use in exchange for stuff I can use. If you want, you can hand out flyers for your local co-op on the way back to the city but in the meantime let me practice a little targeted salesmanship. This isn't Glengarry Glen Ross."

We drove a half-mile down the road and found another subsistence farm on the banks of a fast-moving stream. An entire family turned out there when we drove onto the property, mom and kids with a skinny father whose hands looked older than the rest of him. They were properly dubious when Josh began his spiel but after a while his enthusiasm broke them down. Like any good salesman he directed most of his attention to the mother, emphasizing how effective his laundry soap was and how much time it would save her down at the creek. There was a moment of panic when he mixed some powder into a bucket of water for display and no suds appeared, but he recovered quickly and explained how the altitude kept the bubbles to a minimum – especially useful for rinsing!

"You're shameless," I told him when we headed down the road again. Another forty pounds of fresh beans decorated the back seat.

"Shameless and swimming in coffee," he smiled. "And not just any coffee. This is premium stuff at bargain basement prices. We ought to pack the plane full of it. We would make a killing back in Panama!"

"Not off the guys in the squadron," I replied. "They know what it costs and can come up here and buy it themselves."

"I'm not thinking of the Pinheads," he retorted. "I know people downtown who will gladly pay a premium for what we have right here." He leaned over the seat and counted the bundles, did some math, and nodded happily.

"Something just occurred to me," I said. "If that woman back there rinses her clothes in the creek, won't that soap wash downstream? Do you know if it's biodegradable?"

Josh shrugged. "Not my problem. But you know, something that just occurred to *me* is that I might have missed an opportunity. I didn't sign those guys up. I mean, the logistics of supplying them with product would be hard but maybe I should go back and talk to them about joining the Amway team. They know everyone around here and could be my angle to cracking the local market."

"You want them going door-to-door to their neighbors pushing Amway?"

"Why not? Especially as a family – think of the credibility having a couple of kids along would bring. It could be a business opportunity for them, the kind of thing to break them out of a cycle of poverty."

Far from breaking out of poverty I saw these farmers being shot to death by their neighbors for being annoying evangelists of mail-order schemes.

We went to a third farm but there Josh struck out. The lone farmer on this property had a decent operation with a drying shed as well as a cabin stacked high with twenty-pound bags of coffee, not the one- and five-pound bags we'd seen so far. He wasn't any wealthier than his neighbors, just more organized, and from the start he eyed us with suspicion. He listened to Josh's pitch but grew more disapproving the more he heard. Finally he glanced around at the work he should be doing and delivered an ultimatum that he would sell for cash and nothing else. Josh threw up his hands.

The fourth farm was more receptive. Josh gained another twenty pounds of coffee and was only mildly disingenuous when he promised the couple there that he used the same products in his own home. Which he did – a whole crate of disinfectant propped up a stereo speaker behind his front door.

"You have enough?" I asked.

"No. Let's hit one more."

We drove out of the valley and found a farm at the base of tiny Volcan Morazán. Like their neighbors, the owners there usually took their crop into Chimaltenango or sold it to wholesalers in Guatemala City but they were more than happy to make retail sales to visitors. They stopped work to give us a tour of their property and proudly showed off sacks of coffee stacked under lean-tos near the fields where they grew.

The fields themselves were an overgrown mess. Coffee plants grew in curving furrows over two acres of sloping ground, crisscrossed by chalun trees that protected them from the sun. Coffee also grew behind the house and right up to the walls of the shelters. Everywhere there was an available patch of ground there was a coffee plant. So crowded was it that the inevitable chickens had only a small yard to peck in and so wandered in and out of the undergrowth like tiny piece workers. The farm was a poster child of rural poverty.

Josh walked confidently, sniffing the air and chewing beans. I watched him, knowing he was stalling. There were only towels left in his suitcase – he would have to be on his game to trade them for Arabica.

"Sí!" he declared suddenly, stopping in mid-stride. "This is the best we've seen. The best farm in the region."

The farmers, a father and son, beamed.

"Yes," Josh continued. "This is the kind of operation I've been looking for. I want to expand my stateside operations and this could be the start of it."

Stateside operations? I raised my eyebrow but he ignored me and launched instead into an elaborate explanation of how he had a retail household products business – remotely true – and was interested in broadening it horizontally into an import-export business – not true at all unless he had just decided on it. The father and son listened politely, waiting for the part where someone offered them money.

"Caballeros, tengo algo que es mejor que dinero," Josh informed them.

The son was interested but the father's look made clear he doubted anything was better than money. When Josh pulled out the towels he was more certain than ever.

"Toallas?"

"Ah, but not just any towels," Josh assured them. "These are *Amway* towels."

"Amway?"

"*Sí*. Premium, luxurious, fine Egyptian cotton, Amway towels. You won't see the likes of these anywhere in Guatemala."

"*That's* true," I muttered. Josh glared at me.

"Gentlemen, the founders of my company, the men who first sold these towels are millionaires today. Do you know why? Because everyone wants these towels. Everyone! You will be the envy of Chimaltenango!"

It took a while. The old guy was simple but he wasn't born yesterday. The son, on the other hand, was more inclined to believe in instant riches. He just needed the pros and cons spelled out for him. He touched the towels carefully at the edges and made supportive comments like, "Well, they certainly *seem* luxurious." He even looked to me for confirmation from time to time, putting me in an uncomfortable situation that I squirmed out of by explaining I was really just Josh's driver. They talked it over for fifteen minutes.

In the end what tipped the older fellow over the edge and made him willing to trade his excellent coffee for cheap towels was Josh's assurance that they weren't cheap towels at all and that if he, the farmer, chose to re-sell them himself Josh as a businessman would understand – he wouldn't like it, knowing that he had taken a loss by giving these men an incredible bargain – but he would understand. The farmer could live with that: towels he didn't need, but towels he could sell for a profit he would take. Reluctantly he acquiesced to a deal.

Josh tossed ten bags of coffee into the back seat and motioned for me to get ready to go.

"Gentlemen, *muchísimas gracias*," he exclaimed and shook their hands. "You've taken my best towels at a bargain price but I'll trust you that your coffee tastes as excellent as it smells. We'll have to do more business together."

The son smiled. The father nodded politely, trying to catch up.

We got in and started the engine. The sound energized the father's doubts – he looked at the towels his son held and then at the empty space where his coffee had just been. Clearly wondering what he had just done, he raised a hand to get us to wait. Before he could speak, though, Josh cut him off with a wave and put the truck in gear.

"Vamanos!" he muttered. "He's having second thoughts."

We drove quickly down the hill to the Chimaltenango road.

As we left the driveway a tiny white pickup passed us going in the opposite direction. The troublesome farmer from earlier was in the driver's seat. He didn't look happy. Our eyes met as we squeezed past on the dirt shoulder and he spun in his seat to glower at us as we went by. While Josh steered around some potholes to reach the pavement, I watched the white truck pull into the yard we had just left. The farmer hopped out and had a hurried conversation with the father, who held up the towels.

"Uh-oh," I said. "They're comparing notes. Your customers are becoming self-aware."

The three men waved their arms in our direction. Then they piled into the ringleader's pickup and headed down the driveway after us.

"Aw, no," Josh whined, watching in the rearview mirror. "I hate Indian givers. Hey, get it? Indian givers?"

"Not funny."

"Well, neither are customers who suddenly get cold feet. A deal's a deal."

He got us on the main road and stomped on the accelerator. The truck leaped away, speeding us around a bend and out of sight.

"Great," I told him as we raced down the road. "This is just great. We spend a month in this country learning culture and language and the first thing we do with that education is shaft the locals."

"Don't start with me, Mike."

"Now here we are running like bank robbers trying to cross the county line."

"We won't have to go that far," Josh grinned. "They'll run out of gas before we leave the valley. That's if they can even find us."

He hurried down the road toward Antigua. I caught glimpses of the white pickup through the back window but it fell farther and farther behind. Soon it was visible only when we happened to crest a hill at the same time. To lose them for certain, at the bottom of one hill when we were hidden in a grove of trees Josh turned off the main road onto a lane that seemed to run on a straight shot for the Guat City highway we were trying to intercept. It was a sunken track, hidden by cornfields and pastures, and allowed us to leave our pursuers for good.

Or so we thought. After a mile we came to a Y in the road. Josh pulled over into the grass to study the map but as he did so we heard the sound of another engine. We looked up the opposite branch – only a hundred yards away was the white pickup heading right for us! They were close enough that I could see the driver's arm out his window as he waved an angry fist.

"How the hell did he get there?!" Josh shrieked. "We don't even know where *we* are!"

We raced off down the other branch of the dirt road. It continued west but in our panic to escape we took several turns with abandon. The fields and trees masked our progress and after fifteen minutes we pulled over again to listen. This time there was nothing. I climbed an embankment to look out over the countryside and saw that everything there was peaceful. The only movement came from cattle in a field of clover. A breeze in the ceibas and the buzz of insects were the only sounds.

"Looks like we lost them," I suggested.

"Yeah, maybe," Josh laughed, as lively as I had seen him. The art of the deal – and the run from justice – had piqued his adrenalin and made him slap happy.

"I'm glad you're having a good time."

"Oh, please. I'm not worried about Guillermo and his compadres. A deal's a deal. But if you're that concerned about a little Guatemalan Deliverance we'll call it a day. Too bad – I kind of like tearing up these back roads. Come on, John Dillinger, let's get back on that highway. Let's ride!"

He hit the gas again and we raced off in the direction of the sinking sun. The road stayed dirt, sometimes widening to two lanes as it wound across the highlands but mostly weaving a narrow path between the high grass. Hedgerows hid us and lessened the concern that we would be spotted. They also made it impossible to tell where we were.

"You might want to slow down," I advised. Josh careened around curves so fast I had trouble reading the map.

"You really think there's anyone out here?" he chuckled.

"There's at least one pickup," I reminded him. "Regardless, we can't see what's coming up around these bends. It would suck to turn a corner and drive face first into a couple of donkeys. Remember there's no emergency service out here."

"We'll be okay," he assured me. He slowed passing a farmhouse and then sped up again on the other side. "Besides, this is exciting. You're the one, Mike, who's always looking for adventure. Well, here's your adventure! You're being chased through the middle of nowhere."

"They're not chasing us anymore. We can take time to stop and smell the roses, or in this case the coffee you sleezed out of those simple people."

"Ha ha. There you go again. You know what your problem is, Mike?"

"I'm honest?"

"No, you assume that everybody *else* is honest. You assume everybody in the world is one big happy family."

"I do not. And what does that have to do with you convincing ignorant people that cheap Amway goods are worth the same as their boutique coffee?"

"Ah-ah – you're changing subjects…" The branch of a willow hung over the road and smacked our windshield as we raced by. Josh braked and then accelerated again, kicking up a cloud of dirt. "I had to educate those people. Besides, you don't know. Maybe they needed room fresheners. That's it – maybe it was fate: maybe I got that idea at breakfast because there were people out here who needed a little Amway in their lives. They'll do…"

We turned a bend. The road stopped.

"Watch it!"

"Aaughhhh!…"

It didn't actually stop: it ended in a T-intersection but for us that was the same. Worse, there was a man in an armchair sitting right in the intersection looking at us as we came screaming around the turn. Josh hit the brakes but the car skidded on the loose surface. We smashed into the guy doing forty miles an hour and plowed through the hedgerow behind him. The truck bounced, the windshield shattered, and we came to a stop thirty feet off the road in a pasture of honeysuckle and ragweed.

***

The air smelled of coffee.

"ohhhh..."

The truck didn't have airbags so my face smacked the panel. I was dazed but awake as the engine stalled and the world grew quiet. Dust and pollen floated everywhere.

After a while birds returned to chirping. The meadow buzzed to life. I cracked my eyes open to see a grasshopper fly in the window and land on the dash.

"ohhhh..."

Josh was hunched over the steering wheel. He had banged his head on the roof; fabric there now hung in his face. His hands gripped the steering wheel, the same wheel that had knocked the wind out of him so for the moment he could only groan. There was no blood, not that I could see, though it was hard to tell because of the body lying face-first in the seat between us.

"Oh my god, oh my god, oh my god..."

I released my seat belt and fumbled to open the door, then fell out into the grass.

"Mike, what...who...ohhhh... Oh, no. Oh, no-no-no-no..."

The other door swung open and banged against a tree. There was frantic rustling on the far side of the car as Josh, too, scrabbled to get away.

I tried to walk but fell over in the weeds. A big puff of yellow pollen burst into the air over me. The honeysuckle was in bloom.

"Mike!"

"Over here."

We met at the back of the car. Josh's face was ashen.

"Oh, god, Mike. Oh, god. We hit someone."

I looked back over the tire tracks. We had gone through the hedge like a threshing machine. Splintered branches and leaves were everywhere. The grass was pressed flat; flower petals lay on the down-turned blades.

"*You* hit someone," I corrected him. "I told you to slow down."

"Oh. Oh, that's just great. Spoken like a true friend. Why don't you just take your pocketknife and stab me in the back and be done with it? I can't believe you said that."

"Are you okay?"

He patted his chest and legs.

"I think so. My chest hurts. Oh, man, it hurts. That steering column should have skewered me. You?"

"My head's spinning."

It was. I lay down and waved away a butterfly. Josh put his head in his hands. We had to see about the guy up front but he would have to wait.

"I didn't see him!" Josh finally burst out. "What the HELL was he doing in the road? Are we supposed to be mind readers? We're just driving down a road minding our own business – are we supposed to *know* that some jackass chose today to go out on a blind curve and take a siesta? This isn't my fault! This isn't my fault!"

My vision settled. As it did my eyes picked out more chips of wood scattered in the hedge's remains. There was also color…red, blue, yellow…candles. A pack of cigarettes and a beer can. Something black poked out of the matted grass. A pair of cheap sunglasses.

I rolled to my knees. We were avoiding the front of the car but couldn't delay forever. Maybe the guy was still alive. I peeked around the tail light.

"Mike, wait," Josh pleaded. "No, wait. I'm not ready for this. Oh, god, I don't want to see. We should go for help. His head's probably crushed all over the seat…"

I crept along the bed of the truck. Wisps of smoke rose from beneath the vehicle where our hot engine scorched the grass.

My door hung open. The grasshopper was still on the dash, crouched among bits of broken glass. When I put a hand on the seat he jumped across the body and out Josh's door.

The man lay face down on the front seat, sprawled through the windshield as though impaled on the gear shift. His legs were tucked in a sitting position so that his butt – still outside – stuck up high in the air. A cigar was jammed into the headrest and a black felt hat lay upturned on the hood. Shards of plexiglass covered his tunic. It also coated the red sash at his waist that I first mistook for blood. One of his arms lay on the floor, broken off at the elbow. My heart leaped – then I reached inside the truck and carefully poked the fellow in the ribs.

Josh was still back by the bed, ready to cry. "Is he dead?" he asked.

"It's a statue."

"Oh, god. He is, isn't he? He's dead. I'll be locked up forever…"

"It's a statue," I repeated. "I think we've run over Maximón."

He peeked around the tail lights, confused. Then as the words sank in his whole body deflated, his mind adjusting to the idea that he hadn't killed someone after all. He moved slowly up to the front seat, afraid that I was lying, not putting it past me to put him on even in a tragedy. Then he ducked into the cab.

"You're KIDDING!" came the outburst. "You are fricking kidding me!" He popped back outside and stamped around the front of the vehicle to look at it from that angle. "A statue? A goddamned statue? They put a goddamned statue in the middle of the road?? I thought it was a guy. I thought it was real. I thought my whole life was over, that I was going to be stuck in a Guatemalan jail for the rest of my life for smacking some stupid farmer into kingdom come. My heart…I had a heart attack, goddammit! My heart hasn't started working again yet because I thought my whole life, my whole career was over. Now it's just a statue?"

"Would you rather he was real?" I asked.

"No!" he cried. *"But Jesus Christ!..."*

He collapsed in the grass. I lay down again and watched butterflies.

Finally Josh stood up. Together we walked to the road to see if we could get the truck back out the way it had come in. Once in the intersection it was easy to see what we had done.

Everywhere in Latin America people built shrines by the side of the road. Sometimes they were simple collections of crosses to mark a fatal accident. Other times they were actual shrines, prayer sites ranging in size from a doghouse to a small garage and stocked with statues, crucifixes, pictures and whatever else believers felt like putting in there. Usually the statues were of Mary or Jesus, the ones where she looked like a nun and he a member of a '60s commune.

Guatemala had its own tradition. That was the cult of Maximón. His origins were disputed but he was a mishmash of pagan and Christian cultures, a mock deity who people nevertheless took seriously, a sprite-like figure in dark suit and gypsy garb who peasants prayed to for good luck and blamed for mischievousness when things went wrong. He was depicted standing or sitting but usually the latter, in an armchair like a throne and with a cheesy smile as though he was holding court at a bikini contest. His shrines were repositories of the kinds of gifts – cigarettes, alcohol, chewing gum – that people normally associate with a shiftless uncle. The sunglasses covered wide eyes. The cigar accompanied the leer. A crazed blues master would have felt flattered.

"We went right through it," I marveled, looking at the wreckage on the road. All that was left of the shrine was its stone base. This was the first Maximón shrine I had studied up close but from the extent of the debris the locals counted on this guy for a lot.

"The rest of it's in there," Josh agreed, pointing at the hedge.

We walked back to the truck, picking up pieces of the shrine. At the truck we stared at the statue's butt.

"A foot either way, one of us would be missing a head right now," I commented with a shudder.

"Yeah."

We pulled the statue out of the windshield and propped it against a tree. Maximón still had his drunken smile but his forehead was chipped. The cigar was gone and the tip of his nose broken off. He still looked happy, though, like a frat buddy who's just groped your girlfriend.

"Can we get the truck out?"

I got in and started the engine. With Josh pushing up front I backed it out through the hedge and onto the road. I forgot about the shrine – what was left of it – and drove over the base again. As I did a group of peasants came down the road and stared in horror.

"Lo siento," I told them. "We missed the turn." Josh shooed them on their way.

"We'd better get the damned thing back out here," he muttered. "We can't rebuild the shrine but we can dump all that crap next to it and hope no one notices."

"Yeah, right."

We trudged back into the meadow in search of relics. The shrine was in a million pieces and we quickly realized that the idol itself was all we could hope to salvage. That's when Josh had his breakdown.

Maximón was where we left him, leaning against the sycamore. His one arm was missing but the other was bent at the elbow and pointing toward us. It held a cup that was empty but was obviously meant as a place for people to drop alms. The cheesy grin was disturbing. He seemed to be looking directly at us as though we were all in on the same joke. He struck me as the kind of guy who would see being struck by a car and flying through its windshield as a hilarious stunt. He also struck both of us as someone we should know.

"Oh, my god," Josh stared, realizing it first. "It's Mexican Guy! It's Walt's Mexican Guy."

He was right, of course. It hadn't been obvious with his butt sticking out the windshield but now I felt stupid for not making the connection earlier. Walt's description fit Maximón to a tee with the possible exception that he had been conservative in his portrayal. The main feature Walt left out was the tangible insouciance on the prankster's face. Even bereft of his accoutrements and propped against a tree, the statue ruled the clearing with reckless authority.

I had already been through my experience with The Poet so verifying Walt's dream for a second time, though disturbing, wasn't the shocker it was in Ecuador. I had long since resigned myself to being a pawn in Walt's distorted world. But for Josh this was a crisis of faith.

"Oh, my g... Oh, my," he corrected himself.

We could no longer just drop the old guy back in the intersection. We would have to take him with us. Walt needed a Maximón. Running into him this way, ahem, was just too good an opportunity to pass up. In fact, it couldn't have been an accident at all and I made the mistake of saying as much out loud.

Josh sank to his knees and looked ready to cry.

5

KIDS

Walt had a problem: he needed a Korubo war club. The rest of us had a problem, too: avoiding Walt while he looked for someone to get it.

The Korubo are a small group of Stone Age Indians who live in areas of the Amazon jungle so remote that until the 1980s no one even knew they were there. They're the kind of people National Geographic made its reputation on – small and brown with round bellies, bare feet, and innocent faces that stare into the camera with sullen, cautious eyes. Hunting and sleeping are their primary activities. Loin cloths are their primary wardrobe. They live in isolated bands – isolated even from other Korubo – and are so shy and secretive that the few people who look for them usually come up empty.

Before their discovery they were a rumor, a cautionary tale other jungle dwellers told their children to keep them in line: *"Don't stay out too late, João, or the Korubo cannibals will get you."* Korubo don't in fact engage in cannibalism but since nobody knew much about them the detail wasn't important. Besides, cannibalism wasn't unheard of in the Amazon. The Korubo's real claim to fame – besides being almost extinct – was their reputation for being violent, brutal, and dangerous. Hence Walt's problem.

Being hunter-gatherers, the Korubo are skilled in using blowguns and poison darts but their weapon of choice is their war club. The clubs look like tall walking sticks: hewn poles of Brazil nut or mahogany, five feet long with the thickness and finish of a banister. They lack adornments such as notches or scrolling and have no color unless it's red from the blood of their victims. One could pass as a porch brace or a huge dowel rod to the uninitiated. But supporting a curtain isn't the club's purpose. When stalking enemies the Korubo sneak up as close as possible and then sprint forward with a ferocious cry to clobber their victim's head again and again until the person is dead, the Korubo are tired, or both. Their nickname in Portuguese is *caceteiros*. "Head-bashers."

For almost everything else on his list Walt had a simple, three-step approach for acquiring it: Step 1 – go to that location; Step 2 – find the object; Step 3 – pick it up. There were a few problem items – he had to figure out what Vilcabamba's gold was, for example, before he could go get it – but mostly the challenge was one of logistics, not anthropology or physical safety.

The Korubo war club was thus a unique proposition. First, where were the Korubo? Walt knew they were in the Amazon but that was like saying they were somewhere between the Rocky Mountains and Chincoteague Island. Basic research narrowed their range to a handful of districts in the northern part of Brazil up where the jungles push into Colombia and Venezuela but that still was a huge area. The only town of any size up there was Tabatinga and as a jumping off place for a serious game of jungle hide-and-seek it left a lot to be desired. Further, the Korubo don't live in towns or villages. They live in clearings in the jungle, in clans of eight to thirty people in straw huts called malocas. They migrate unpredictably. They don't trade, they don't travel, and they don't move about in the open. Granting that Tabatinga was halfway to nowhere already, how was one to find anybody below the canopy of the densest, least explored jungle of the world?

Second, the reason the Korubo were so remote was that they liked it that way. It wasn't in their DNA to be social. They weren't the kind of people who sat around a campfire and wondered where everyone else was. They were the kind of people who sat around a campfire and said, "You know, this morning I heard a strange noise way off to the south. Tomorrow let's move ten more miles to the north." Anyone who came near them usually did so by accident because they didn't realize the Indians were there in the first place.

Last, while the Korubo could be kind and loving to each other and even generous (though wary) toward strangers, they were subject to wild and indiscriminate mood swings. The warrior who was leading you down a path to a fresh water spring might suddenly whirl around and crush your skull with his club. *Just because.* The female who moments earlier invited you to share a seat by the fire might abruptly thrust a spear into your chest. *Just because.* Strangest of all was that neither the warrior nor the woman would have had any intention of doing those things just seconds earlier. Bipolar didn't begin to describe them: random is more accurate. Korubo acted on the spur of the moment and those moments oscillated from one emotional extreme to another. Even the rare visitor who gained their trust long enough to observe their daily activities was wise to depart camp before nightfall: if Korubo were scary during the day, who knew what darkness might inspire?

Simply put, few people had ever heard of the Korubo, fewer had actually seen them, and nobody understood them. Their infrequent encounters with the modern world were with either the *sertanistas*, Brazilian forest rangers, or with miners, loggers, or hunters who encroached on their territory. When the *sertanistas* encountered them it was deliberate since the *sertanistas* needed to know where the Korubo were in order to keep other people away from them. When miners or loggers or hunters encountered them it was an accident. Each year the latter pushed farther into remote corners of the jungle in search of wealth. Each year some of them encountered the Korubo and the encounter was always violent – the Korubo usually killed at least a handful of the interlopers. Survivors brought back horror stories to the rest of us.

So when Walt realized he needed a war club belonging to one of the most remote, primitive, and violent people in the world he was quick to apprehend that he wasn't the right person to go get it. Neither were his usual volunteers in such matters – the rest of us in the squadron and wayward souls such as Vince and Harry. No, this search was beyond the mere abilities of irresponsible aircrew with a yen for adventure. It required somebody infinitely more irresponsible. Irresponsible, but also capable, determined, and likely to have been described in his high school yearbook as the person most likely to say 'Hey, watch this,' as his final words. In short, Walt needed an operator. It wouldn't hurt if the operator was also crazier than a loon.

***

Rob Wells wasn't crazy but he was impulsive and stubborn. That's why he agreed to go. At least that's what we guessed because we couldn't come up with anything else. Either that or he was crazy.

Rob was a pararescueman in the Howard detachment. He was a tech sergeant, a borderline-crusty enlisted man who had been around long enough to understand that your career can be successful *and* fun only if you work at it and carefully define your terms. He shared the common PJ traits of enthusiasm, confidence, and a short attention span and added to those a dose of mule-headedness that often kept him digging a hole long after he should have climbed out of it. Like any good operator he preferred action over reflection. As a result he spent a lot of time asking forgiveness of the same bosses who earlier would have denied him permission to do whatever he was apologizing for. He apologized a lot.

Rob had been in Panama for a while but spent a lot of time not on operational status because of the regular injuries he suffered. Just in the time that I knew him he contracted dengue fever, pneumonia, and malaria, broke an ankle during a parachute jump, fractured a rib falling out of a fast boat, dislocated a shoulder wrestling a caiman, and nearly drowned during a night dive off Portobelo. He wasn't a fool or incompetent – he just pushed things to the limit more than most and bore the scars to prove it. We learned that the worst thing to say to Rob was something like, "These clouds are too low to jump," or "The water's too cold for this dive." It only encouraged him to go and find out for himself.

Despite his foolhardiness, everyone in our squadron liked Rob because he was the kind of guy who would sidle up during an exercise and say something like, "We're going to be shooting off a bunch of surplus ammo this afternoon. You interested in helping out?" or "You ever been in a RHIB before (a Rigid Hull Inflatable Boat)? We're testing a new one on the Chagres this afternoon – might see some rapids if you want to come along." Unlike most ground-pounders he didn't hate aircrew, seeing them as coddled, indolent whiners. He looked past that and saw instead coddled, indolent whiners who had a sense of adventure. Also, we weren't averse to ignoring rules. Rob discovered that when he found out how we were getting into our remote fields when the weather was bad – by descending through the clouds until we broke out or hit the trees, whichever came first. Not that Rob was one to buck the system for the hell of it. Unlike Walt whose assault on regulations came from a desire to prove they weren't well-thought-out in the first place, Rob accepted that people needed limits. He just had trouble defining them.

Where that character came from no one knew. He was born to academics near Stonehenge in England and Charlie Manson believed that a neighborhood Druid had swung by at his birth to curse the child into becoming a thrill seeker. Maybe, but his parents didn't stay in England. They moved him to New Zealand for most of his childhood. That's the land of perpetual kid-behavior, the nation that invented bungee-jumping, jet boating, and rolling down hills in a large plastic ball. It's possible some of the local restlessness rubbed off. While his parents taught, Rob climbed glaciers, skied from helicopters, and swam in ice-cold fjords. He was proud of his youth on the South Island and considered himself part-Kiwi.

Master Sergeant Wolverson, the senior PJ, described Rob as driven. Wolverson's boss, Captain Bolrok, agreed and noted that Rob had more focus than anybody he'd ever worked with. He usually went on to add that a bull in a ring has great focus, too, right up until the matador skewers it.

What I knew about Rob came from Big Bud (who met Rob at the water survival course) and from small-talk around the squadron.

His path to the military was roundabout. After moving to America as a teenager and becoming a citizen Rob applied to all of the military academies with the goal of joining the special forces. But each school turned him down because his grades weren't good enough. He almost got into West Point anyway on a rugby scholarship – the New Zealand national team, the All Blacks, were his heroes – but the week before his final interview he broke a leg during a match and his opportunity came and went.

Hoping to wait a year and try again, he did what a lot of guys do and went to a military prep school for a year. Prep schools, though, are hit-or-miss: it's hard to keep your eye on the goal when you've already been told once that you're not good enough and when the goal isn't guaranteed to happen, anyway. After excelling for several months, Rob's stint at a school in Tucson ended when he was busted for organizing the junior students into a game he invented called Deer-Beer. (It combined gambling, drinking, and hunting within the city limits.) It was Rob's way of relaxing after hitting the books but the school administrators didn't see it that way. They kicked him out. The road to the academies grew hazy. He no longer knew what he wanted.

He enrolled at a community college but left after a while. He sold cars. Then he moved furniture. More jobs followed. He coached a rugby team, built trails for the Forest Service, taught skiing in Flagstaff, and opened and closed a judo academy. He drifted. He moved to L.A. where he raced motorcycles and also tried his hand at acting. He did stunts on shows like *Knight Rider* and *The A-Team* and earned minimum wage as an extra in crowd scenes where he mouthed "watermelon-watermelon" to fake a real conversation. He lived paycheck to paycheck. For a time he lived "outside" – his euphemism for being homeless.

By his own account, Rob only began to gain focus when someone set fire to his truck. One night after a race in Riverside he was on the shoulder of a highway asleep in the front seat of his pickup when the bed exploded in flame. His racing bike was back there along with cases of motor oil and high octane fuel. The bike, the truck, and all of his belongings burned to the ground. He was lucky to make it out alive.

For months he assumed that the fire was an accident. Then he found out that a fellow racer, a gang-banger named Chaco, had deliberately set the blaze. For the first time Rob's outlook on life crystallized. For the first time he wanted something really, really badly. He wanted revenge.

His friends urged him to re-consider: Chaco was a Crip. They feared that if Rob did anything to him the whole gang would hunt him down and leave his body in pieces along Highway 1. But Rob was undeterred. In fact he was emboldened by his attacker's membership in a gang. If the Crips wanted him to back off that only made him more determined to have his way.

He searched for Chaco for weeks. He went to every bike race he could find. He haunted the hoods of East L.A. and combed police lockups. It took a while and he had to range farther afield than he expected but finally there were enough clues to point him in the right direction. When he found Chaco his lust for revenge was at its peak. Rob was not only ready but impatient to vent his fury on the hoodlum with all the violence that his head-butting, judo-throwing, rugby-mashing past allowed. And he almost did.

But then the situation stopped being cut-and-dry. Chaco had quit his gang

Worse, he had quit the Crips and gone clean. Not just clean but spiritually clean. Monkishly clean. A gunshot wound, a drug overdose, and the pleas of a pious relative caused Chaco to experience a religious conversion and change his lifestyle for good. By the time Rob found him he had dropped out of the Crips and devoted himself to poverty, prayer, and spiritual renewal – he had re-established himself in a Cistercian monastery in Oregon.

Even for someone as headstrong as Rob that was a dilemma. Not religious by temperament, he still understood karma. Chaco had changed. Something in Rob told him that he should, too. Maybe he wasn't supposed to ride bikes. Maybe he should move in a different direction away from racetracks and interstates. He reconsidered his desire for revenge. Could he kill a monk anyway, he wondered? We all do stupid things when we're young, after all. Most of us don't commit arson and attempted murder, granted, but on a relativist scale was that dumber than Rob picking off an eight-pointer as it grazed by a suburban front porch? Kids will be kids, he told himself, and eventually we all have to grow up.

After much soul-searching he decided to let sleeping dogs lie. He left Chaco alone and returned to L.A.

But then another fire swept through his campsite. It was a natural blaze caused by lightning and had nothing to do with gangs, Crips, or motorcycle racing. But it torched everything he owned for a second time and left him once again sitting in the dirt on an empty hillside contemplating the stars and his place in life. With no one to blame, Rob took it as a sign: To hell with sleeping dogs and their Trappist isolation and to hell with karma – finish what you start. He went back to Oregon, broke into the monastery, and beat the crap out of Chaco. Then with the entire Crip nation on his trail he fled east and joined the Air Force.

The Air Force made him a cop.

Rob wasn't thrilled about that and he wasn't thrilled, either, when the military returned him to California for his first assignment – to Edwards Air Force Base, out in the middle of nowhere. His mission there was to patrol the vast desert boundaries of the service's test center and watch for interlopers sneaking onto the site. It wasn't an exciting job so Rob did what he could to make it more interesting. One day while driving the perimeter he tried to repeat the slalom action he had perfected on motorcycles and in doing so rolled his pickup down an arroyo.

Rather than just call it in and apologize, though, he got on the radio and made up a story to cover his incompetence. He reported how he was in hot pursuit of a trespasser across the farthest reaches of the base. His plan was to describe a dramatic chase that culminated with him wrecking the car and the bad guy getting away. Unfortunately, he got so caught up in his own story that he was still on the radio giving a play-by-play when the reinforcements showed up. There he was, sitting on his overturned car, screaming into the radio "I've almost got him! I've almost got him!" while his sergeant looked down from the top of the ravine.

He got in trouble for that but one good thing that resulted was that when his enlistment was up the cops didn't want him anymore. If he wanted to stay in the Air Force, they said, Rob had to cross-train.

He applied to be a gunner on an AC-130 gunship but wasn't picked up. He tried to get into the Office of Special Investigations but OSI didn't want him. At the last minute his career adviser suggested the para-rescue world. With his records he wouldn't have made it under normal circumstances but that year the timing was right: the Air Force had enough cops, enough gunners, and enough special agents, but not enough stubborn, muscle-bound, independent thinkers with a penchant for trouble. So Rob became a PJ.

He did well in the rescue world, at least according to his own value system. He wasn't political nor was he astute about moving through the ranks but he did get several rescues under his belt. That built his confidence and his pride. He also got to travel. He did tours in England, Iceland, and Japan before coming to the Canal Zone. Those experiences let him see how other people lived and how other cultures regarded him, something that became more important as he matured and tried to find his place in the world. For the most part foreigners thought well of him and he thought he knew why: unlike many gringos abroad he didn't mind wandering far from the safe confines of American settlement. That comfort came across to the people he met. He still felt lost occasionally, not sure where he was from or where he belonged, but he made up for it by focusing on others and trying to figure out who *they* were and where *they* belonged. He knew that so long as he was himself he would have no problem dealing with the natives.

Now if only he could mesh with the Air Force.

The PJs were the perfect place for Rob. As far as he was concerned, anything that didn't involve being outdoors, testing one's strengths, and taking risks was a waste of time. That wasn't a unique sentiment in the rescue world but it meant that 80% of what we did in the military – bureaucracy and paperwork – was pointless to him. *That* was a problem because as he became senior in rank that 80% occupied more of his time. He tried to forestall it by ignoring it but that just brought him counseling sessions with Captain Bolrok and more time at a desk. Wolverson warned Rob that if he didn't hunker down and fill a few management squares, tech sergeant would be as far in the ranks as he would climb. But Rob found it hard to get worked up over that. It wasn't rank he needed.

Which is why the Korubo war club piqued his interest.

***

If you're on the ground, there's no easy way to get to Tabatinga. Even in a boat or an airplane there's no easy way. Just to get close you have to travel all the way to the northeast corner of Peru where the jungle squeezes up against Colombia and Brazil. Tabatinga isn't as remote as Iquitos but it's smaller and the people who live there view even their fellow Brazilians as people from a far-away place.

We flew to Tabatinga on occasion. The arrival there was a challenge since there were no navigational aids and the runway itself was in horrible shape. Tall plants stuck up through the concrete and trash lay about the ramp. The river port was just as bad. It was the main way people got to or away from Tabatinga but you wouldn't know it from looking at the warped piers and splintered pilings that passed for berthings. In fact, because of the shifting currents on the Amazon River the port rarely stayed in the same place for more than a few seasons. One trip you might disembark on one side of town, the next on the other.

What Tabatinga had going for it was that it was just downriver from a Peruvian town called Leticia and so benefited from that town's trade and popularity; what it had going against it was that it was in Brazil and a philosophical world apart from the better organized Peru. Where Leticia was poor but proud, 'Tinga was a dirty, sprawling shantytown that reeked of river mud and bad manners. Whereas Leticia called itself the "world center of peace and prosperity," in Tabatinga peace and prosperity were in short supply. The economy sucked, its authorities were corrupt, and daily rains made the streets open sewers. Disease was common, crime was rampant, and poverty was a given. All outsiders were targets from the moment they set foot on shore.

For those reasons I thought Rob might like the place.

But I misjudged him. Though the idea of a Korubo club *piqued* his interest it didn't seize it entirely. When Walt explained the quest Rob thought it was dumb. He expressed no enthusiasm to take part and in fact said that it was much ado about nothing. About his task in particular he had reservations. Not about the danger – that was a plus.

His concerns leaned more toward the practical: after all, he couldn't just nip down to the Amazon over a weekend and go exploring for a lost tribe. It could take weeks, months – even the Air Force would notice he was gone. And how did he find the Korubo once he got to Brazil? What would the Brazilians think? And who would feed his dog while he was gone? It seemed to be a lot of work for a stick. Mrs. Wells didn't raise a total idiot – notwithstanding her son's yen for adventure, in his opinion the club was just a club. Go buy one somewhere, he told Walt.

But the end was never in doubt. Walt could sell tanning oil to a coal miner so convincing Rob to go walkabout in the Amazon was just a matter of time. It comforted him to know that Rob never worried about the physical dangers of the trip, like being killed and eaten. He also took comfort from the fact that the SEALs occasionally went to Brazil, too. He hooked Rob up with them – and then put himself on a trip south to make sure he got to Tabatinga first.

***

The SEAL team in Panama had a frustrating role in our theater. Although technically they existed in case the SOUTHCOM commander ever needed a bunch of door-kicking commandos to take down some bad guy, in reality they spent their time traveling around the hinterlands trying to make friends and influence people in the name of nation-building and international relations. Frequently they teamed up with some host nation's river patrol units – known as "riverines" – and did "friendship exercises" where the two forces lived and camped together for a while to share expertise. The locals liked it because they got the bragging rights of saying that they worked with American

SEALs. The SEALs hated it because they were bored silly. In their minds it was like tasking Rambo to spend quality time with Boy Scouts.

Aside from their wounded egos, though, a practical effect of their travels was that the SEALs knew a lot of people. That included a riverine patrol based at Tabatinga. It was on one of their trips south that Rob tagged along.

But that trip was a disaster. The Brazilians that month were mad at the Peruvians over shipping rights on the Amazon River so instead of being available as promised for an exercise, the riverines spent the entire time intercepting cargo ships headed from Iquitos to Manaus.

Rob and the SEALs endured torrential rain and clouds of mosquitoes while they sat on their butts doing nothing, waiting for the riverines to quit shaking down barges like a dirty cop in the week before Christmas. Rob caught pneumonia. Two of the SEALs contracted schistosomiasis. The team leader, Dave Penny, fumed. He argued with the Brazilians and got nowhere. They told him to go back to Panama; he swore his team would never return.

***

But it was while they sat around watching the rain that Rob, desperate for something to do, enquired about the Korubo. To his surprise, as soon as he did the local cops tracked him down and told him to keep his questions to himself. Then the border guards joined the effort to shut him down. Both groups had been tipped off by Walt that some "crazy adventurer from the States was on his way" and they responded like the East German Stasi guarding state secrets. The border guards even made a special trip to the port building where the SEAL team had set up quarters to warn Rob that travel into prohibited areas was, well, prohibited.

He blew off the warnings and kept nosing around for info on the Korubo. Finally the cops arrested him. The Brazilians locked him up and readied to throw him out of the country, which was exactly the wrong thing to do (and exactly what Walt wanted) because now Rob's mulishness replaced his indifference about the Indians: whereas before he mocked the search for a club, now he vowed to lead the whole tribe of Korubo up to Times Square just to rub it in the border guards' face. He was only released once the SEALs intervened and promised to keep their PJ under control.

***

Yet despite the hoopla around his questioning Rob learned nothing about the Korubo until he caught pneumonia. It was then that he met someone useful.

Fernando, his doctor at the Tabatinga hospital, was a jovial MD and a frustrated plant biologist from the University of Sao Paolo. He was in the region to do research in the Yavari Basin and had permission from the *sertanistas* to be on stretches of the Yavari River normally closed to travel. But he had two problems. The first was money, specifically the lack thereof. Without funds he had no boat, no supplies, and no cash to hire guides. His second problem was security. He had no one to accompany him into the interior since the Yavari was Korubo territory. Until the funds materialized he was working at the hospital but he really wanted to get on the road. Hearing that, Rob became the man's best friend.

That led to his second trip south, a trip that began in Iquitos where Jem and Big Al dropped him off when they flew down for our normal hub-and-spoke mission. With the Brazilians mad at the Peruvians and the riverines mad at the SEALs (and the border guards mad at him), Rob couldn't get the customs officials to approve his entry into Brazil at Tabatinga. So he tried to cross the border elsewhere. Following questionable tips from locals he caught a boat going south out of Iquitos up the Ucayali River. He was told that the Ucayali would take him to a feeder river across the frontier in Brazil, thus avoiding customs. It didn't. Instead his excursion turned into a survival exercise when the barge ran aground three days south of the Amazon. He had to walk and raft his way back to Iquitos, living off jungle tomatoes and river catfish that he caught with his hands. Two weeks later when Jem and Al were ready to return to Panama, Rob showed up at the plane with a bad case of the runs and a refreshed appreciation for mosquito netting.

Months passed. Fernando found funding and Rob did more research. On his third try he got closer. He flew to Leticia, paid off the customs officials, hitched a ride downriver, and hopped on a speedboat with the biologist and two mixed-race locals, *ribeñeros*, who Fernando hired as guides. But only an hour out of Tabatinga they were fired on by bandits from the river's shore.

"They do that," the biologist explained. "If you look like you have money they do that."

The bullets punctured the boat's gas tank. They also scared the *ribeñeros* who quit their jobs on the spot. Now the group would never make it upriver and back. So they turned around.

Rob's fourth trip was the charm. When the dry season rolled around and farmers around the region set fire to the countryside to clear away brush, massive blazes flared up in northern Brazil and threatened the villages of the same people who had set them. Our squadron was tapped to help the Brazilians move aid to the more remote locations. On one such trip Rob hitched a ride with us directly into an overgrown airstrip north of Tabatinga. From there he walked to the river, threw his gear into the repaired boat, and they took off.

When he and Fernando reached the same point on the river where the bandits had fired on them before, the bandits fired again. Only this time Rob was ready. It was now almost a year that he had been trying to get to the Korubo and his tolerance for fools was short. He pulled an M-203 from his bag – the M-16 with a grenade launcher attached – and fired back, strafing the shoreline and blowing down a few trees for good measure. The bandits fled.

"Ha-ha!" the biologist cheered. "You can come with me more often!"

After that, they drove up the Yavari undisturbed.

The Yavari River led to the Itacuai. That river led in turn to a smaller waterway called the Itui, its entrance hidden among paxiuba trees that crowded its banks, black water flowing between their roots.

Along the Itui the jungle closed in on both sides, the foliage so dense it dragged on the boat. The water shallowed. No sound came from the foliage beyond insects and birds. The river wound in oxbows that sometimes had them running parallel to the Itacuai and feeling they were making no progress. Then it turned inland, its width varying as it lost the characteristics of a river and became instead a flood plain soaking the jungle floor. Rob stood at the bow and directed Fernando when the obvious course disappeared. The biologist slowed the boat to a crawl.

When it seemed they could go no farther the river narrowed again and deepened. It still coursed right and left but now the impenetrable forest broke to offer glistening sandbars on the outside of turns.

Above the sand were clearings where sunlight reached the ground. Although the bars proved to be quicksand, the clearings allowed a sense of perspective to the otherwise choked shores. Even Fernando, no stranger to the jungle, expressed his delight.

At dusk they rounded a bend to find one more clearing, their destination. A clapboard cabin stood in its center. It rested half on the ground and half over the bluff where poles held the structure and a deck above the water. The same poles supported a pier beneath which were a pair of canoes. It was the *sertanistas'* base camp.

***

They stayed for three weeks. It took half that long for Rob to convince the resident *sertanista*, a lithe, bearded man named Fabio Belho, not to send him home. Belho had nothing against Rob but the whole point of his job was to protect the Korubo from anthropologists, missionaries, and adventurers. Rob was just such a tourist.

But the irony was that after all his efforts Rob had no desire to see the Korubo. After a year of reading about them he had begun to respect how they lived. He liked people who did their own thing and as far as he could tell that's all the Korubo were doing. If they wanted to be alone, he figured, leave them alone. But he still wanted a club. If Belho would bring him one after one of his irregular visits to the tribe then Rob was content to sit on the *sertanista's* pier and swat flies.

Eventually Belho was willing but it took a while. The ranger limited his visits to the Indians, in part because he didn't want to contaminate their culture and in part because the Korubo weren't always where he expected them to be. Sometimes he and his bodyguards, a pair of Matis Indians who spoke little but who could read the land like a large-type postcard, would travel for days and find no sign of the elusive natives, leading Belho to fear that the clan had retreated into the jungle. Sometimes they would find only empty huts where a dozen people had been living just a month earlier. Then they would pass by the same sites later and find everyone in place as though they had never left. The Korubo never explained their departures and Belho didn't press for answers. One of the frustrations of his position was that while he had a duty to protect the natives, often the best way to do that was passively – staying away even when he wanted to visit and deliberately remaining in the dark about their activities while the scientist in him desperately wanted answers.

So for days Rob hung around the cabin doing nothing. He was curious about the Korubo but not enough to pressure Belho. Instead of trekking through the jungle he spent his time reading books and playing backgammon with the Matis. He had come too far to get impatient now.

***

But while Rob was being stoic, Fernando was working. He had no interest in the Korubo at all. The fact that they lived in proximity to the plants he studied was in his opinion an inconvenient coincidence.

Fernando was in the Yavari Basin to study the iporuru plant, a species that he believed had potential for development as a cold medicine. Iporuru grew in the Itui watershed so the good doctor was in botany heaven, leaving the cabin each morning to wander in the woods and search for specimens. He was also a bit stressed because rainy season was coming. The plant disappeared underwater when the rains came so he roamed farther and wider every day to find good samples before that happened. Rob or one of the Matis often accompanied him since when Fernando was on the hunt he paid no attention to anything except the ground cover at his feet. He had no time for snakes, spiders, or natives unless they could help him find his plants.

It was on one of those early mornings when Fabio and his bodyguards were gone, when fog rose like steam from the Itui's dark surface and rain frogs grumbled from the leaf litter, that Rob heard crashing in the forest and a scream of pain. He leaped from the pier to investigate.

Fernando raced back down the trail toward the cabin. He had a pencil-length dart hanging from his face above the left eye, a decoration that flopped and spun as the scientist ran all-out, frightened out of his wits. He tried to pass but Rob grabbed him.

"What happened?" he demanded.

What happened was that the dart, the diameter of a cocktail straw, had penetrated the skin beneath Fernando's eyebrow and passed on through, spending its poison on the bushy hairs therein. Though his left eye and the muscles around it were already relaxing like a wilting flower, the scientist himself was otherwise unscathed. Unscathed but petrified. And he had reason. As Rob pulled the dart free there was a noise up the trail.

"Run!" Fernando gasped, and bolted for the cabin.

Rob turned to find the dart's owner, a Korubo warrior, in full sprint down the trail. His blowgun was nowhere to be seen but his club was. Raised high, it and its owner were intent on catching up to Fernando. The warrior was surprised to see a second person in the trail but it didn't slow him down. With no hesitation he altered his stride and with a blood-curdling cry leaped straight at Rob, swinging for his head.

Rob stepped aside, ducked, and clothes-lined the Korubo. The Indian somersaulted backwards and crashed to the forest floor unconscious.

***

When Fabio returned that night he found the Korubo duct-taped to a piling. Rob stood guard with his M-16 – he expected other members of the tribe to come looking for their warrior.

Fabio insisted they cut the man loose.

Once free, the Korubo rubbed at his skin, somewhat shell-shocked. The Matis spoke to him but he didn't answer. He merely eyed Rob and then moved carefully out into the darkness.

When the *sertanista* heard the day's events, he was thunderstruck. Fabio's job was to establish an understanding with the Korubo regarding non-Korubo. The fact that most of his "understandings" usually lasted only as long as it took the Indians to have a change of heart made this attack no less disturbing. His challenge now was to disentangle the day's events from his own diplomatic efforts to prevent lasting damage to what little relations the two cultures had.

He came up with a plan to deal with the incident but waited three days to let the Korubo calm down. Then he shared his idea with Rob and Fernando.

"I want you to come with me to the tribe."

His hope was that by arranging a meeting he could convince the natives that the scientist and the white man meant no harm. If everything went well it might dissuade the Korubo from attacking people in the future.

Fernando said hell no. He was dead set against seeing his attacker again. He had come within an inch of having his skull bashed in and wasn't interested in making peace with the man who tried to do it. Besides, his research was going well: he had two coolers filled with plant roots and was ready to return to the university and put them under the microscope. Fabio could settle the frontier without his help.

Rob also said no. A Korubo club had literally fallen at his feet so he, too, was ready to call it a day and return to Panama. But his real reason for backing out of the visit was more prosaic: he really didn't want to see the Korubo. He wanted them to stay unspoiled.

"I read some of your books," he told Belho, "Let's leave 'em alone."

Belho gave in. He knew his idea was a long shot. He agreed that his two guests should leave and resolved to find another way to rebuild trust with the Indians.

Two days later Rob and Fernando packed up their boat and headed down the Itui. Fabio and his men accompanied them as far as the confluence with the Itacuai. Patches of sky seen through the canopy were gray and the gloom of the forest was deep as they pushed out into the river. The air smelled of rain.

They had drifted with the current two miles when a clearing formed by a cuipo deadfall appeared on the bank. Standing wide-legged and impassive among the fallen branches were three Korubo warriors.

"*Opa!*" Belho muttered. He waved cautiously to the Indians. They didn't respond but Belho chose to interpret their lack of overt hostility as a positive. Since the river would take them within feet of the natives anyway he waved both boats ashore. His Matis guides held their rifles ready.

The Korubo had tan skin and thick hair cut in a mop top around the head. Their shoulders were broad and their arms muscular but their quick legs and short stature gave them a top-heavy look common among many creatures of the forest who need strength, speed, and the ability to move in choking foliage to survive. It made the scowls on their faces seem deeper. They carried bows and the omnipresent club. Rob noticed the Indian who attacked him standing in the back of the group: he had a new club.

"Kuwa," Belho greeted the Indian closest to him. The man regarded the *sertanista* darkly.

Belho hopped ashore. He greeted each of the Korubo by name.

"Don't make sudden moves," he advised Rob and Fernando while watching the natives. "But don't back down, either. The Korubo will try to intimate you."

They succeeded with Fernando. He shrank before the Indians' glare. Rob rose to the bait and locked eyes with Kuwa.

Kuwa listened as Belho, with the Matis translating, introduced Rob and Fernando and expressed his pleasure at seeing the natives. But then Belho berated them for their attack on the biologist. When he did that Kuwa's expression changed to defiance. He interrupted Belho and spoke for some time.

"The short story," Belho relayed, "is that there has been a misunderstanding. They did not know you were here, they did not know you were with me. Also, you surprised Te-wan while he was hunting." He nodded toward Fernando's attacker who didn't look the least bit apologetic. "It is all your fault," he said, and then hastened to add, "I mean, it is all my fault. The point Kuwa wishes to make is that attacking you is not their responsibility."

Fernando wished to debate that point but Rob shrugged. He remained seated on the biologist's boat and watched the Indians with a poker face. His M-16 lay on the floor – beside Te-wan's club.

There was more discussion between the ranger and the Korubo and then between the Korubo and the Matis. It appeared to cover a range of issues. Some of it obviously touched on the incident days earlier because the Korubo turned frequently to look at Rob. Finally Belho turned to him in exasperation.

"They want to know what you did to Te-wan and why you didn't kill him. He doesn't remember anything after he attacked you. I've told them you are a great warrior from our culture but they don't believe me."

Rob laughed at that. "Nobody *ever* believes I'm a great warrior," he said. "I tell people all the time and they never believe me."

Belho didn't share in the humor.

"It would be better if *these* people believed you," he cautioned. "They don't fear warriors because they are warriors themselves. But if you are not a great warrior then you must have some kind of magic that allowed you to defeat Te-wan and erase his memory. If you have magic that means you are dangerous enough that they should kill you."

Rob stopped laughing.

"I like the way they think," he commented.

He stood up and stepped ashore, his eyes on the lead Indian. Rob was thin and wiry so it was hard for him to intimidate anyone but he stood tall and faced forward. "Tell him I am a great warrior," he instructed the Matis. "Tell him I will fight him right now, with or without weapons, to prove it."

"No, don't say that," Belho countermanded him before the Matis could speak. "Weren't you listening? If you do that we'll have a fight on our hands and the Korubo don't fight for fun. If you fight, you will have to kill him or he will have to kill you. I don't need that."

"Then what do you want me to do?" Rob muttered, still bowed up.

"Don't you have a good story you can tell about how many men you killed, or a war song to sing?" Belho asked.

"Uh, no."

"Then make one up!"

Fernando grunted skeptically from the boat.

"My experience with the American military is slight," he observed, "but to the best of my knowledge war songs aren't part of their arsenal."

Rob took his eyes off Kuwa long enough to regard the forest ranger and agree. Then he thought about it.

"How about a dance?" he asked the *sertanista*.

"I beg your pardon?"

"Do you know what a haka is?"

"The Maori haka?" Belho replied. "I can't tell you much about it."

"I know all about it," said Rob, who had grown up watching the All Blacks use the aboriginal war dance to intimidate their opponents. "Would they like to see one?"

Belho studied him closely. "I like the way *you* think," he said.

He informed the Korubo that to demonstrate his warrior nature Rob would show them the traditional dance his people performed before they went into battle. It was *just* a demonstration, he emphasized.

"Not all hakas are war dances," Rob corrected him.

"This one had better be," Belho retorted.

Rob stripped off his shirt and adopted a wide-legged crouching stance at the edge of the clearing. He glared at the three warriors before him who spread out to watch. They glared in return but their stolid expressions were tempered with curiosity. Rob's chest was no broader than their own and lacked their healthy complexion. He didn't look particularly dangerous.

But then Rob unleashed a terrifying cry and leaped into the air. The Korubo stepped back.

"Fabio!..." Fernando whispered.

"Relax, doctor," the *sertanista* urged.

Rob leaped again and waved his arms. He pummeled an imaginary opponent, beating him to a pulp and making slashing motions with his hands. He continued to jump, moving side-to-side only yards from the Korubo, going high and curling his feet under him as he slapped his chest and thighs and shouted unintelligible threats in the language of the original Kiwi. His eyes bulged, his face contorted. He twice came close to Kuwa and stuck out his tongue. The Maori were cannibals and the tongue gesture was meant to warn rivals of their fate after the battle was over. Kuwa knew nothing of the Maori but cannibalism was familiar enough. He grasped the imagery and clung to his war club fiercely, refusing to be bullied.

Rob's dance lasted only a few minutes but he made the most of it. He beat his chest until it was red, shouted himself hoarse, and in one final motion made a lunging motion as though to rip out his enemy's heart. Then he dropped back into his crouch and glared at the Korubo in silence. The clearing echoed with his final yell.

Fernando was terrified. The Matis were impressed. Even Belho didn't know what to make of the scene, wondering if he had risked too much. For a moment nobody moved.

Then Rob stood up and flashed a big smile at his opponents.

"Was that enough?" he said to Kuwa. "Or should we fight now?"

One of the Matis translated his words before Belho could interrupt. Kuwa stared at Rob a moment longer, perhaps wondering what in the world he should make of this bold but skinny white man who was trying to intimidate him. Then he laughed out loud. His companions joined in. They rested their clubs on the ground and began to talk animatedly among themselves and with the Matis.

"They believe you are a warrior in your land," Belho said after listening for a while. He was much relieved. "But they are not afraid of you. They say you jump around like a monkey."

"So?"

"So, they eat monkeys every day."

***

Back in Panama Rob presented the club to Walt and told his story. Since none of us had ever seen a haka we prevailed on him to repeat his performance from the clearing. He did but reminded us first that its meaning lost something when done in a living room filled with drunken aircrew rather than a jungle setting complete with armed Indians. The sense of imminent mortal combat, he pointed out, didn't translate well.

"But I don't understand something, son," Jem asked. "That Tewan guy expected you to kill him. When you didn't he wanted to know how come – what did you tell him?"

Rob nodded. His eyes fixed on something out the window. It wasn't hard to imagine him contemplating how many things in life he had to worry about without the additional weight of killing a man whose primitive innocence outshone anything he had ever done.

"I told him that as a great warrior I prefer to let sleeping dogs lie," he said finally. In response to our puzzled looks he added, "I don't think that translated well, either."

6

Vilcabamba

Camp Drinkalot was Don Redelkite's discovery. It was a beach low on the Azuero Peninsula accessible after three hours on the highway and ninety minutes on gut-busting dirt roads. Don was one of our pilots who discovered it from the air one day, on a low-level when he and Evan crossed the coast and saw waves breaking in close sets over a sandy bottom that rippled for miles along a deserted shore. Don was a surfer and thought the place had potential as a location for his own endless summer. He vowed to see it on the ground.

He didn't go alone. On the first trip six of us drove out. We went prepared to surf (though only Don knew how). What we didn't go prepared for was the beach's isolation.

There were no houses, no fishermen to ask directions, and the nearest village was four miles up the coast. The only fresh water was a creek. It was the boonies.

Thankfully we brought a small canopy to huddle under for shade, two bags of chips, and beer. A lot of beer. In fact, the only thing we had in great quantity was beer. For a day and a night we did nothing but drink, surf, and chase blue crabs.

It was a gorgeous location, a paradise of bright sky, sand, and waves that rose before the green of the jungle to reflect its hue.

Don threw his board in the water and within minutes was riding waves. The rest of us paddled futilely against the currents. We counted ourselves lucky if we caught a wave at all, much less stood up on the board while doing it. I remember once scrambling like mad alongside Story Earnhardt for an hour straight, both of us determined to get through the breakers that washed us back with laughing indifference. Eventually we never got anywhere and had to turn around, so exhausted by the effort we could barely stand even in shallow water.

"The ocean hates us," Story declared, and it was hard to disagree.

But it was because of the ocean's hostility that we remember Camp D at all, because that's where Evan had his revelation about Vilcabamba's gold.

On one plunge into the water he broke through the surf after fantastic effort and managed to catch a small swell. He stood up but immediately fell over and was rolled along the bottom of the bay by a succession of larger waves and the vortex they generated under the surface. When he finally reappeared he had almost drowned. The sand on the bottom was rough and riddled with seashells. He'd found rocks, too, so he was beaten, bruised, and his shorts were shredded into a loincloth. Being drunk didn't help. When he retrieved his board and paddled in, he was exhausted.

"White-blue, white-blue, white-blue, and green all around. That's all I saw," he reported to us, gasping on the beach. "The white was the sky, the blue was the sand, and the green was everywhere else. Weird. Not what you expect to see underwater. And the weirdest thing was that I've seen it before."

"What do you mean?"

"I mean, it *felt* like I had. Big time déja vu. Only not there. Somewhere else."

"Another beach?"

"No. Not in the water." He pointed to the sky. "Up there."

"White clouds, blue sky," I offered. "You see that every day."

"White clouds, yeah. But the sky's above them, not below. When have you ever looked *down* to see blue?"

"All the time over the ocean."

"Yeah, but that's not it. I have a feeling, Mike, and it's got something to do with that Vilcabamba guy. Don't ask me why, but while I was down there rolling along all I could think was, "Nobody would ever see this from up above." I should have been worried about drowning but instead I was thinking, "Nobody would ever see this from above.""

"What does that have to do with an old Inca running from the Spanish?" I asked.

"I said, don't ask me."

Evan was the nicest guy in the world. Because he was so calm and deliberate by nature we had to take his intuition seriously, even when he spoke of the last item on Walt's list.

***

"What do you think it means?" Walt asked me one afternoon.

I shrugged. "That the treasure is in the ocean somewhere?"

"No, definitely not."

"How are you so sure?"

He waved his hands over his head, his way of saying that he just was.

"It's in the mountains."

"But white-blue-white-blue...what does that mean? White could be clouds, or an overcast sky, or maybe a fog bank. Blue's got to be the ocean. Green, of course, is jungle. Is the treasure somehow above the clouds? Or maybe the white is for sand. Maybe Evan had his up and down mixed up. Maybe it's not in the ocean but near it, or out in the desert somewhere or on a beach. Jeez, that would suck. There's about four thousand miles of beach on the west coast alone."

"It's not in sand," Walt said. "It's not on a beach."

"How do you know that?" I demanded and waved my own arms to ask if that was his answer.

"It didn't come from the desert in my dream. And there's no desert in your photos."

He was right about that. I'd forgotten about the wall map from La Recoletita. We had studied Maj Plunkett's photos for weeks after our return from Bolivia. But the writing was indecipherable and the map features too vague. After innumerable guesses, theories, and attempts to relate the picture to a real-world map, most of us gave up. Only Walt and Mystic Pete still plumbed the picture for information, meeting regularly to talk geography and grid lines. They had resolved that it showed Peru but that was it. And Walt was right: there was no sand in the photos.

"And it didn't come from the beach," he continued. "Whatever the hands were holding up came from the mountains."

"The mountains aren't blue, Walt. There's also no jungle up there."

"There must be."

"But..."

"It's up there, Mike. Whatever it is it's up there."

"But where?"

He didn't know.

***

But there was one person who did. Charlie Manson, of all people – who believed Walt's dream was due to drinking too much of Perry Trapazzano's beer – stumbled on that person one afternoon at the end of a Peru hub-and-spoke. Flying home from Iquitos, he and Kurt Norris dropped into the town of Borja to escape a ring of storms that threatened to wash them out of the sky. There they found a clue.

Borja was a jungle settlement of maybe five hundred people. It sat twenty minutes east of the Andes on a bluff over the Marañon River and was so unremarkable it blended into the terrain like a leaf on the forest floor. Its sole distinguishing feature was a wooden church. Most churches in the basin were plaster and concrete because wood was eaten apart quickly by insects, but not the church in Borja. The Borja church was all wood right down to dowels and pegs. Not a bit of metal held it together yet it sat on the same rain-soaked soil as every dilapidated, mildewed house in the village . For some reason it was impervious to nature's appetite. It had stood for as long as anyone knew and was as solid and sturdy as the day the first joist was laid. The only metal feature in its whole construction was the stainless steel cross atop the steeple and that didn't count against the church's feat because it was added to the building in the mid-1970s. The church was a jungle miracle.

The cross was the only reason any of us knew Borja existed at all. On sunny days it glinted like an airport beacon and could be seen for fifty miles. On daytime flights we used the flash as a check on our inertial navigation system while cruising back from Iquitos – even Josh called it his Star of Bethlehem until I reminded him that the last guys to follow a star ended up Christian.

Next to the church a woman sold bread and crushed fruit drinks from her kitchen window. With nothing else to do while they waited for the storms to pass, Charlie and Kurt sat on her steps eating bread and drinking punch and watching lightning dance around the jungle.

After a while they noticed that someone was watching them watch the storms. An old man in the door of the church rocked himself back and forth on a homemade chair and studied them like he would be tested later. When out of sheer boredom Charlie talked to him, the fellow said he had a message for Walt.

But it took the boys three weeks to remember to pass it on.

"You *what!?*" Walt shrieked when Kurt casually mentioned the incident at a squadron picnic.

"I forgot, sorry. He didn't know you by name, of course, but he said one of our friends was looking for something from a dream so I figured it must be you."

"Oh, you figured that out all by yourself, you genius? Moses appears to you in the desert and points the way to the Promised Land and you simply make a mental note to tell the rest of the tribe *three weeks later??* What the hell were you thinking, Kurt? God damn it. *Charlie!!*"

Charlie was non-plussed.

"It's your stupid dream," he sniffed. "Not mine."

***

Walt put himself on the first plane scheduled down to Peru. The mission went but got caught up in a flurry of cargo runs between Lima and Chiclayo and despite his best efforts he was never able to cross the mountains before the AOC ordered him home. I tried on a later trip and so did Mark Jonkris but it was a month before Mike Vaneya was the first among us to have the guts and opportunity to land at Borja for no official reason. When he did, he returned with bad news.

"He's dead," he told us. He threw his gear on the ops desk and wiped sweat off his forehead with both hands. Pressure from his headset made red ovals around his ears.

Walt stood up in shock. "Dead?" he demanded. "How can he be dead?"

"Well, he was pretty old from the looks of it. Died yesterday morning. His son was there – even showed me the body, not that I cared but it seemed to matter to him. Said the old man was waiting for you."

"He doesn't know me!" Walt protested.

"The kid said he did."

"Oh, please. I would remember. And he won't get a chance now."

"Well, you stood him up. I guess he got tired of waiting."

"How did *I* stand him up? Couldn't he have called?"

"From Borja?"

"A letter, then. They must have mail. He could have sent me a damned letter if he was so anxious." Walt glared around the room, seeking answers. This was another setback and he wasn't sure how to take it. When his eyes met mine I had to shake my head. I had long since stopped trying to explain his Twilight Zone world.

"It's a strange place," Mike continued. "Borja. They were all standing around when we landed, like they were expecting us."

His co-pilot, Lowell, walked in and nodded. "Must have been pretty disappointed to see us and not the Chosen One," he added. "What kind of religion waits for Walt as their savior, anyway? Idiots."

Walt tapped the desk and stared at them.

I felt sorry for him. Of all of us he was the simplest – pilots like to brag that if it isn't small words and short syllables we don't want to hear it, yet Walt made even that outlook seem complex. The guy lived to fly. Period. Now here he was trying to absorb some paranormal riddle and at the same time face the unpleasant and inconvenient fact that our only clue to its answer was currently a guest at his own Peruvian wake. It was too much to swallow.

"He's not dead," he announced.

Mike chuckled.

"He's dead, trust me. I saw the body. From the looks of it the guy was a hundred and fifty years old as it was. No wonder he gave up. You should be grateful he stuck around as long as he did."

"Well, I'm not grateful!" Walt barked. "If he's been around that long he could have waited another couple of weeks for me to tweak the schedule. And if that damned oxygen thief Manson ever thought about anybody but himself I would have been down there in time as it was!"

Walt pulled the original list out of his pocket and studied it. He had been chasing his dream for over a year. Like most of us he started the quest thinking it a game, then over time graduated to dutiful participation as it turned out that the seemingly romantic items like war clubs and rain sticks were, in fact, just war clubs and rain sticks. But then a funny thing happened. A lot of us changed as a result of one or another part of the search. Rob Wells found peace. Mark Jonkris found a woman. Even Lowell broke out of his misanthropic shell long enough to take one for the team. Lee Plunkett discovered a cause in dirt-poor children, Johnny Luca overcame his shyness, and Josh – *Josh* – after finding the culture of Maximón reached back to his own family roots and was on a slow but sure path to becoming an Orthodox Jew. Even I wasn't immune. Though I was in my own way as cynical as Lowell, Lisa and her poems made me wonder if somebody's natural order hadn't been riding along in my cockpit all those times when I should have crashed. None of the search made sense but it had begun to take on an air of destiny. If so, who was I to stop it?

Not everyone's take on the hunt had evolved the same way. There were other theories. Some still thought it was about gold or at least the potential for money. Little Bud thought it was an elaborate con. Griswold thought it was idol worship. People began to argue over which discovery was more valuable and who had worked harder to recover an item. Evan went off in his own direction and began to worry, thinking that maybe we weren't supposed to find all the items and that if we did in fact uncover Vilcabamba's gold the event would trigger some cosmic event like an earthquake, a flood, or Walt being raptured. He joined Charlie in urging that we quit while we were ahead.

Walt didn't worry about being raptured. In fact that might have appealed to him because it would have given him an opportunity to ask the Big Man for a better flying schedule. Not counting on such a celestial event, though, he worried instead about being worried and not knowing why he was. It wasn't that he was scared, it was more that he was anxious he might fail. So far the quest showed no sign of completion. After a year we weren't any closer to finding Vilcabamba's gold. Some guys were already looking at moving on to other assignments and leaving Panama. The last thing Walt wanted was a damned treasure hunt hanging over his head for the rest of his life.

"He's not dead," he repeated and threw Mike's helmet bag back to him. "He can't be. I'm going down there to prove it."

***

But he didn't get down there. Not for a while. Every time he tried something happened that even Walt couldn't control. First we were activated for hurricane relief in Honduras and everyone had to relocate there for a month. Then the C-130 side of the house and most of our leadership decamped to Rwanda to participate in a belated national statement against the genocide there. While they were gone we restricted operations to Central America. Then we had a readiness inspection that stopped all our operational missions and made us focus for three weeks on check rides, currency flights, and updating the regulations. Finally, Walt caught a cold that wouldn't go away. It wasn't until the middle of September and the full onset of the rainy season that life settled back into its normal routine and the scheduling board held trim, predictable lines of sorties, crews, and destinations.

"Mike, we're going south," Walt informed me one day. He could no longer wait.

"It's about time. Where? When? For how long?"

"Iquitos," he said. "Friday." He stared at the board as though he could see the jungle in it. "For as long as it takes."

We flew to Iquitos. It wasn't a destination Walt particularly liked. He loved to fly but he wasn't an explorer at heart. Whereas Josh soaked in the gritty isolation of jungle towns like a bar rag sucking up spilled booze, Walt looked on them as puzzling anachronisms. When we weren't flying between radar sites he spent his time in Iquitos sitting at a table at Ari's Burger, wondering why the inhabitants of the town didn't leave and go somewhere with paved streets.

Only when we flew to Borja did he lighten up.

"Nice town," he commented as we landed, dropping out of a rain-washed sky that sparkled against the mountains. The church flashed by on our right as the landing gear kicked up spray from puddles. "For a developer, anyway. It wouldn't be hard to increase the value of this place. You could tear down all these huts and put up condos overlooking the river. Or just tear them down and do nothing."

Nobody waited for us as they had for Charlie and Kurt. We walked from the runway to the church and didn't see a soul. The cross dazzled above us, reflecting the intermittent sun.

"Nice church, too," Walt conceded as we peeked inside. The interior was dim, the pews empty. The altar was bare except for a waste basket and a vase of blue flowers. "Not musty like everywhere else."

We closed the door and moved on. The village was deserted. Our loadmaster, Luz, called *Halloooooo* to get someone to open their door but it appeared there was no one inside the huts to comply. Only when we headed back to the airfield did a human being appear, a lone man who walked up a path from the river and waved as though he had seen us five minutes earlier.

"Hola," he said. He was plump and unremarkable but had a friendly face. He pointed toward the church to indicate we should join him walking back there. The movement was so natural that we did it without thinking.

"Hello," said Walt, swinging into stride alongside the man. "Who are you?"

The man just looked at him so I translated.

"You've come for my father," the man replied. "I am glad. He's waiting for you."

"Alright, now look..." Walt started and then caught himself. He took a deep breath. "Who was your father?" he continued with elaborate effort. When the man didn't answer he added, "Everybody keeps saying he was waiting for me but I don't know who he was."

I translated but the son wouldn't bite.

"He's waiting for you," he repeated.

Trying my own tack, I asked, "Where is everybody? Down at the river?" I pointed behind us toward the path the guy had come up.

"No," he replied. "They're waiting, too." He pointed ahead of us to the church.

"No, they're not," Luz spoke up. "We just came from there." The tone of his fluent Puerto Rican Spanish neatly conveyed his belief that we were wasting our time. He wanted to be back in Iquitos where the ladies awaited his return the way showgirls in Vegas used to await Elvis.

"Esperan," the man insisted. "They're waiting."

"Lo que sea," Luz muttered. Whatever.

We walked the rest of the way to the church in silence. At the steps we kicked mud off our boots and swung open the door.

The place was packed.

Thirty people standing in the pews turned to look at us as we stepped across the threshold.

"Where did they come from?" I demanded.

Nobody answered. Luz waved his hands in front of him to say he wanted no part of any of it and retreated to the road. Walt frowned. He looked at the people, looked outside, then back at the people. "Strange town," he agreed.

Our companion walked down the center aisle to the altar and picked up the waste basket, which turned out not to be a waste basket at all but a cardboard container with a lid. He ignored the flowers but in the light from the doorway they defied him and pierced the gloom of the church with their rich color. I realized they were the same flowers I had found with Sandy in Otavalo. Blue gentians. Supposedly rare and found only high in the Andes, but here in the sweltering jungle there was a bouquet that would dazzle a peacock. I was so surprised I didn't think to mention them to Walt.

The son carried the box to us. It was wrapped in twine tied in a bow, looking for all the world like a to-go order of fried chicken, and he handed it to Walt with as much ceremony as a take-out order deserved. As he did this the people in the church followed his movements with their eyes. Several shuffled in place and one man coughed, a happy reassurance that they weren't ghosts or figments of my imagination, but no one said anything. They just watched. When Walt accepted the box a murmur of contentment rippled through the crowd.

He hefted it, unsure what to do.

"What's this? *Qué es eso?*"

The son gestured as though it was obvious.

"Es mi padre."

Walt dropped the container. The son caught it and handed it back but Walt refused to take it. They pushed back and forth.

"You must take him."

"No!"

"Sí!"

"No!"

"Sí! He goes with you."

"Why? Where?"

"Can we do this outside?" I interrupted. The people in the pews were giving me the creeps.

We went out to the road where the son pressed his case.

"He was waiting for you," he insisted. "He wanted to go with you so you must take him."

"I don't even know who your father was," Walt enunciated carefully, slapping me on the shoulder to translate. "I don't know who he was, I never met him, and I have no idea why he was waiting for me. I thought maybe he had something to tell me about something I'm looking for. That's what we hoped. But now he's gone. Did he tell you? Did he tell you what he wanted me to know?"

The man shook his head.

Walt sighed and kicked the mud off each of his boots in turn, only to put his feet back down onto the red-brown soil and pick it right back up. He looked at the empty houses like they were properties he couldn't rent out and considered what to do. The two nearest buildings had mold growing up the outside walls. The owners tacked corrugated tin sheets over holes where the wood rotted away and the mold even grew on that, forming peaks of green fuzz that stretched up four feet from the ground. He looked back at the church where not a spot of mold was in sight. The walls there were so dry they could have been slapped together by Ikea two days earlier.

"What do you think, Mike?"

"I assume that's filled with ashes?" I asked, pointing to the box.

"Unless the guy was really short." He shook the container before I could stop him. The sound of – well, the sound had nothing for me to compare to so we guessed it was ashes – came from inside. The son's cheery face didn't waver.

"Um," I stalled, hesitant to ask the obvious question. Luz came up then and asked it for me.

"*Oye, mozo*. You got ashes in there?" he asked the son. "*Cindras?*"

The son nodded. "*Es mi padre,*" he repeated.

"What are we supposed to do with him?" Luz demanded.

The son gestured with his arm toward the plane.

"I thought so," Luz nodded. Ever the loadmaster, he took the box from Walt, set it down on the porch, and yanked the twine free. If we were even considering putting the container on the plane, Luz wanted to see for himself what was inside. He flipped the lid and took a look. Then he swirled the contents around and looked closer. The Peruvian's lips went tighter but he kept quiet.

"Okay," Luz said in English. "Looks like a campfire to me."

Walt leaned over and took a peek. I did the same.

"You'll take it on the plane?" I asked.

Luz shook his head and snorted, the action making his oval figure jiggle. For someone who was normally protective of everything Hispanic he was being unexpectedly dismissive toward a fellow Latino's loss. But I reminded myself of two things: Luz had never thought much of Walt's treasure hunt, and Borja was a long way from San Juan. "Yeah, sir, if that's what you guys want to do. It's just a box to me. But I don't know why you want to. What are you going to do with it, huh? And why does this guy want you to take dear old dad up to Panama? *Oye, hombre,*" he barked to the son, and repeated his question to him.

"*No, no. No va a Panamá,*" the son corrected us. "*Va allá.*" He turned and with a sweep of his arm indicated the Andes in the distance.

"*A dónde?*"

"*Allá,*" he repeated.

"Where in the mountains?" I specified.

But he turned and went back inside the church.

***

"Here's my plan," Walt announced over the intercom an hour later as we flew high over the foothills. "We just find a spot somewhere before the crest and dump the old guy out. That way he gets into the mountains like his kid said he wanted, but he's still on the right side so on a sunny day he can look out on the homestead down there in Borja."

"I can't believe you took his ashes."

Walt sucked at his Seven Dwarves coffee mug and wriggled against the lumbar support of the seat.

"Why not?" he asked. "What were we supposed to do?"

"Say no."

"Oh, please. We come all the way here, find out the guy is not only dead but ready to be scattered to the four winds, and the son says he was waiting so he could get us to agree to drop his remains in the mountains. How do you say no to that? In fact, *what* do you say to that? Damned if I know. But don't worry. This is good PR, a good deed for the locals and it doesn't take us out of our way."

He tried to sound cheery but I wasn't fooled.

"You're as creeped out about this as I am," I told him.

"I am not."

"Yes, you are. You're acting all Mister Wild-and-crazy pilot, we'll-just-fly-into-the-mountains-and-scatter-some-guy's-ashes as though it's no big deal, oh and it's a nice thing to do for the locals and besides it answers your questions about what the guy was doing down there and why he asked for you. No, it doesn't! It doesn't answer anything. You've got him on board because you didn't know what else to do and you know how I know? Because I didn't know what else to do, either, and you're just like me. You couldn't come up with a good reason to say no to that guy without feeling guilty so here you are with a creepy box of ashes and not a clue what we're doing."

He toyed with the straw for a minute and then threw the empty mug on the floor.

"Yeah, you're right."

We didn't know what to do but we had a lot of gas, an empty cargo hold, and a decent day for flying so we flew around for a while thinking about it.

The rains from the jungle had marched on the mountains before we got there. By the time we arrived they were gone, leaving in their wake wet air and wispy stratus layers that overlapped each other like baffles on a ceiling. The baffles were always there. On most days they capped the mountains and hid the peaks, masking the upper reaches of the Andes in a mantle of creamy white. On the rare occasions when they were gone, they didn't so much leave as drop out of sight, collapsing into the highest valleys in the form of dense fog. That left a great photo op for people at the coast but for those of us flying over at 20,000 feet the picture straight down remained implacably opaque.

Today, though, the wind shifted beneath the baffles. Now that the storms were gone it blew uncharacteristically from the west and pushed the lowest moisture back where it came from. Squeezing beneath the clouds but across the tops of the mountains, air flowed like water cresting a dam, scouring the valleys and arcing over the foothills in a long, smooth wave that stretched as far as the eye could see. Clouds – not the baffles hanging above but those masquerading as fog at the surface – were washed off the Andes for hundreds of miles, a waterfall in the open air. As an ensemble picture it was so thick and solid and slow that from a distance it seemed not to move at all. But when we got closer we saw the frothy apparition flowing – floating – as though in an invisible channel three miles above the earth. Meteorologists called the air movement a mountain wave but this was the first time either of us had ever seen – or heard of – it mixing with cloud vapor to become visible to the naked eye.

Walt steered us behind the swell and parallel to the Andes. Mountain waves could rock a plane hundreds of miles downrange of a mountain and this one soared gracefully over miles of foothills before curving down toward the jungle. From there it began an undulation of Amazonian proportions before vanishing on the horizon. So long as we stayed beneath the opaque wave, in a tunnel of air that we would never have picked out from cruising altitude, we were safe.

"Wow," I commented. "Have you ever seen anything like this?"

The tunnel continued as far as we could see. The stream of air above us flowed from left to right, its underside the uniform white of everyday clouds. The otherwise sunny sky disappeared.

Walt glanced up, unimpressed. The physics of the wave mattered to him, not the aesthetics.

"No."

"I feel like a fly on the back side of a waterfall," I said anyway. "Nothing but foam on two sides and an entire mountain range to explore on our left."

"Lovely. Just keep the water over there. I'll worry about the mountains."

"Where do you want to drop this guy, captain?" Luz asked, nudging the container with his foot.

"I don't know, Load. Someplace close. Maybe up there."

"On that ridge?"

"Yeah, or on the back side. I don't know. It doesn't matter."

"Then why not right here?" I called him out. "What are you waiting for?"

We flew inside the wave until the entrance behind us was lost to sight. Walt eventually turned around and climbed higher in the foothills, then dropped into a series of linked valleys running north-south with the cordillera. They were gorgeous, remote areas, rocky and barren, too high for human habitation and without a road in sight. We discussed a variety of places that looked as good as any other as a place to spend eternity – Luz even climbed down into the cabin to be ready to open the ramp. But each time Walt decided to wait. He let me depressurize in anticipation but wouldn't say what I knew he was thinking. He wanted a sign.

But the sign didn't come and after a while we realized we had to do something. Walt settled on his original plan of spreading the ashes where Borja – or its cross, at least – was still in sight. He popped out of the valley we were in and banked left to cross over the ridge.

"Luz, you're cleared to open. We're high, though, so keep the oxygen close."

Behind us Luz secured himself to a gunner's belt and hit the switch for the ramp. The latches clunked up and the door rose. Sunlight streamed through the cabin.

Out of nowhere a cloud sucked us in. The view outside disappeared.

"Whoa, where did that come from?" I asked, instinctively grabbing the map.

"I don't know," Walt snapped, momentarily discomfited. When Walt flew, accidents didn't happen yet somehow he had just accidentally put us in a cloud. Instinctively he started a climb. "One of the stratus layers, maybe. I've lost the ground on this side. You have it out the right?"

"No, nothing." If we stayed popeye we would have to climb and return to the coast IFR. "It's all....wait. Wait, I've got something."

The layer on my right began to shred. We had just left a clear, windswept valley, after all, so if I could get the ground in sight we would be safe to descend back into it.

"Nothing but cloud back here," Luz called from the cabin. He stood on the ramp, the box of ashes at the ready.

"Stand by, Load. I've almost got it..."

The cloud thinned, then broke into a wide fissure that revealed unmistakably the valley's floor a thousand feet below.

"I've got it! My controls – coming down and right."

I pulled power and slid us down through the fissure. Immediately we popped into the clear. But the valley we entered looked a lot different from the one we had just left.

It was bluer.

"What the hell?..." Walt asked, leaning forward to look over the nose. "Is that rock?"

The valley was wide and long. Its walls were covered in forest but pitched steep and built high so they poked up into the clouds everywhere we looked. Their angle made the floor they flanked seem even flatter than it was. And it was flat. Runway flat, with only a narrow creek splitting off a section of the ground near the east wall to give the rest of the surface perspective. It was also covered in a sea of waving blue flowers.

"Is this a farm?" Luz asked. He leaned against his gunner's belt to see below. From that angle he couldn't even see the valley's sides. Everything in his view was the valley floor, an enchanting and confusing sight.

"I think they're gentians," I said, not knowing what else to say. "Blue gentians."

No sooner were the words out of my mouth than the plane lurched in turbulence. We heard an *"Oh!"* from the back.

"Luz? Luz?"

"What was that?" he replied.

"A thermal. Just turbulence. You okay?"

"Yeah, I'm fine. But we just buried the old guy."

Walt and I twisted in our seats to look back. Luz stood at the ramp with empty hands.

"You dropped him?"

"I didn't drop him! You guys... Okay, I dropped him. But I wouldn't have if you could fly straight."

Walt took the controls and banked into a hard turn. Behind us and far below we made out the cardboard container tumbling through the air, its top gone and drifting behind it in a lazy free-fall. A pale cloud expanded above the two of them, the ashes dissipating like steam from a kettle. When our wingtip vortices settled into them they swirled even more and finally settled on the waiting flowers.

"Damn," Walt muttered. "I don't think that's what the old guy wanted."

"There's no way to know," I replied.

"You can't see Borja from here."

"Nope. You can't see anywhere from here."

"I wanted him on the ridge. This valley is hell and gone from anywhere."

"Yeah, but he can hardly complain. This is...something." That was an understatement. Hundreds of acres of blue flowers filled our windscreen. "From what people say, these flowers are rare."

"Who cares? That guy in Borja is going to be mighty unhappy, that's all I know. He said the mountains but I think he wanted Pops closer than this. He'll bust a gut if he tries to visit."

"No kidding," Luz added, now sitting on the ramp with his feet dangling in the slipstream. "Look at that jungle. This must be one of those cloud forests. You can't climb through that. And he can forget about flying in. We got lucky today but with this weather nobody would ever see this from up above."

His words were a thunderclap in the cockpit. Walt and I stared at each other. Then we looked outside – up, down, and at the walls of the valley, finally seeing the obvious. *White-blue, white-blue, and green all around...*

"Find a runway," Walt ordered. "We're going to land."

***

He angled toward the side of the valley and began a turn.

"Huh?" Luz asked.

"Find a runway. We're landing."

"Walt,..." I started, wondering what to say. There was no runway. But he descended and now the blue flowers were everywhere in the windscreen, their sumptuous panorama blocking my thoughts. It was impossible to tell where the flowers stopped and the ground began. "We're almost 10,000..."

"I don't care."

"There's no strip. If we wreck..."

"We won't wreck."

He set us up smack in the center of the valley a third of the way along from where we had dropped through the clouds. The walls bowed there like the sides of a Greek pillar and curved inward again two miles on.

"Can we just do a flyover first?" I pleaded. "Let's see what's out here before we plop it down and hope for the best."

Walt agreed but it was more due to the realization that there was nothing in the middle of the valley to look at than because of safety. He kept the speed up and we droned to the end of the valley where it narrowed. The trees came down to meet the flowers there but we didn't see anything of interest before being forced to turn around.

"Hold on, I've got something," Luz announced.

"Where?"

"We went over it in the turn. Looks like a shelter. And there's something back in those trees."

Walt flew an oval to return on the same ground track. Luz ran up to the cockpit to guide us in. We didn't see anything in the trees but the first object came into view near them – it was a lean-to of sorts overrun by the gentians and with one wall a hillock ten feet high. A side of the lean-to was open. Just before we had to turn again we all got a peek inside.

"What the…?" My mouth dropped open. "Did you guys see that? Was that what I thought it was?"

Walt banked left and slapped the dash repeatedly.

"Gear down!" he called out. "Gear down, gear down, gear down!"

We flew back toward the middle of the valley and reversed course once more to line up on the hillock. Even in a hurry Walt wouldn't short himself on landing distance.

At 10,000 feet any plane needs a lot of room to fly itself onto the ground. I lowered the gear and flaps and watched out the window as the flowers below turned from a seamless mass into individual plants that raced by with startling speed. They were so thick that even when I looked straight down I didn't see soil. What would we land on, I wondered?

We landed on flowers. The ground below them was firm but we never felt it except through the crushed resistance of thousands of plants that our gear mashed into the earth. Walt touched down on a beeline for the hillock with hardly a sound.

"Wow. Let's see you do that anywhere else," I challenged him absent-mindedly.

He grunted. He sat rigid in his seat, peering high over the windscreen as the C-27 decelerated and drove itself through the meadow. Walt was more nervous than I'd ever seen him. Not only had we just landed in a field in the Andes in the middle of nowhere, but we had no idea what we would find when we hopped out of the plane. Luz summed up the atmosphere in our cockpit.

"So this is what it feels like to be on another planet," he commented.

The C-27 rolled to a stop a hundred feet short of the shelter. We sat there while Walt stared out the window, deciding what to do. He let the engines idle but their deep-throated rumble was absorbed into the carpet of flowers. For once the din of the compressors seemed more like the purring of a large cat. Even the usual vibrations were cushioned by the plants matted beneath our wheels. The props swung over endless blue petals, waving the stalks this way and that and blowing some up into the air where they flew slow, cartoonish arcs before settling to earth and disappearing into the ranks of their brethren.

"Shutdown checklist," Walt announced.

***

Luz hopped out to watch the props spin down. When Walt and I joined him he coiled up his comm cord, wading through the gentians.

"You want to get the guns out?" he whispered. The setting inspired quiet.

"No," Walt answered.

"The ground looks good. We could probably turn around and take off the same way we came in."

"Okay."

The valley was huge from the ground. Huge and striking. Its colors came from an artist's palette and I wished Evan could be there to see them. Cloud forest covered the hills in a jade ring. The sky over them was pearl.

The gentians stood so high we couldn't see under the belly of the plane. They were staggeringly beautiful, a blue so deep we could have been resting on the surface of a lagoon. I plucked a flower from the closest plant – it was as remarkable as the first one I'd seen in Otavalo. Sapphires on a stem. In Ecuador a small vase of them had seemed exceptional. Now uncountable millions of such wonders spread far enough for the C-27 to take off and land twice. The bracing smell of the bouquet was a whole atmosphere of pure Andean air pulled from the earth. It was sweet and fresh and so clear that we could see butterflies hundreds of feet away, dipping and weaving above the blooms like student pilots in tiny planes.

Tiny planes. I turned and saw Walt and Luz already halfway to the hillock, pushing their way through the flowers. I ran to catch up to them.

"It is," Walt said as we rounded the hillock. "It's exactly what we thought."

The lean-to was built on the hill's downwind side. It was sturdy, all wood, and had been there some time as evidenced by gentians from the hill growing over the roof. The cover clearly worked because the Ford Trimotor parked inside was in excellent condition.

"Would you look at this?" Luz exclaimed. He circled the machine and exclaimed its condition.

The plane sat nose-high as all tail-draggers do, showing an optimism and enthusiasm to fly that tricycle-gear craft never manage. The three engines – one on the nose, one on each wing – were clean and rust-free. The propeller blades were solid. The corrugated aluminum that covered the body and the wings likewise was intact. Beaten and faded but intact. Control cables ran down the outside of the fuselage and were tight. The tail was straight, no birds nested in the intakes, and all the doors swung on their hinges. The rubber molding around the windows was dry but the glass itself was in one piece. We could even read the gauges on the side of the wing engines. I peeked in the cockpit and saw that the original instrumentation was still there. The cabin had dirt and twigs – mice had run amok but without seats and wall padding they had nothing to chew on. For a plane that was sixty years old it looked alright. Not museum quality but alright.

A path led through the flowers toward the trees. Walt stood at the top of it with his hands on his hips.

"What do you think?" I asked him.

He eyed the aircraft considering how to react. "I don't know," he said. "It's cool, I guess. I just thought...I thought there would be something more obvious."

"Like what?"

"I don't know. A guy named Vilcabamba, maybe, sitting on a pile of gold."

"You said you thought there wasn't any gold."

"I don't know what I think. All I know – and I'll say this for the eight hundredth time – is what was in the dream." He stared at the plane and shrugged, like a polite child accepting a Christmas present he doesn't really want. "That wasn't in the dream. But it's cool."

"It's cool, alright," I said. "Harry would go nuts over this plane. When I tell him about it he's going to start planning a trip up here for himself."

"Why?"

"Why? Because it's a piece of history. The Trimotor was Ford's big contribution to aviation. It was the first all-metal plane and was about as safe as they got for that age. Henry Ford threw a lot of money at aviation for a while which gave designers and manufacturers a chance to push forward. Most of all, by putting his name out there in the industry he helped convince the public that aviation was something they could trust. I mean, he was Henry Ford, the maker of the Model-T. If he built planes like he built cars they must be okay, right?"

"The Ford Company built this one?" Luz asked. He poked his head into a rear hatch to peer upward into the cabin where his voice echoed through the interior. "The same guys who built my Escort?"

"Yep. I don't know the specs but this plane had power and range. Lots of drag because of all this," I ran my fingers across the ridged surface of the left wing. "But like your Escort it was cheap and reliable. That's what Ford did best. This plane could carry people and stuff and didn't crash very often. That was a ringing endorsement in 1930."

Luz closed the hatch and patted the elevator. Down below, the tail wheel squeaked in response. It was a tiny ring of solid rubber on a caster and normally would have been rock-solid, but now it had play because the main gear were missing. The struts sat instead on two wide logs that were none-too-steady themselves. Another pair of logs blocked the open sides to the structure as though to keep the plane from rolling out.

"Where are the wheels?" Walt wanted to know.

I shrugged and Luz shook his head but someone else answered the question for us.

"Inside," a soft voice said. "I couldn't keep them inflated."

***

We all jumped.

An old man on makeshift crutches stood behind us on the path. He leaned on the sticks, one leg cocked and held off the ground. From the knee down it was wrapped in a splint.

"Jesus H. Christ!" Walt exclaimed. "Who are you?"

The man, tall and stooped with pallid skin, raised an eyebrow. He pulled a bandanna from a pocket and dabbed at his face.

"I'm the fellow who owns that plane," he answered.

He hobbled forward. Walt backed away but the man's interest wasn't in him – he stared at the C-27. "I thought I was dreaming when I heard you fly over. It's been sixty years since anybody landed in this valley. In fact, you're only the second plane *ever* to land in this valley." His gaze slid eagerly over every panel of our plane. "That's a nice bird. I hope you have better luck getting her out of here than I did."

My mouth dropped open.

"You've been here *sixty years?*" I asked.

The man looked at me like I was an idiot.

"Oh, hell, no. Who do you think I am, Rip Van Winkle? It gets cold here, son. Real cold. You're high up, you know."

"I know. Sorry, I just thought you might be..."

"What?"

"Somebody else, that's all."

"Like who? What's your story, morning glory?"

"Me? I don't have a story."

"Then what are you doing here?"

"I...we...he..." I pointed to Walt.

"What's your name?" Walt demanded. He watched the old man as though expecting him to vanish at any moment.

"None of your business," the man replied. "You ask a lot of questions. I was here first. Who are you? You drop out of the sky and scare the wits out of an old man – you in trouble? Something wrong with your plane? You running drugs?"

We introduced ourselves.

"Panama, hey? Whoah, I haven't been there in a long time. How's the Canal going?"

"Uh, good," Luz answered. "It's finished."

"It was finished when I saw it, too, genius. But I hear they've got a bridge now. Is that so? How's that working?"

"The Bridge of the Americas?" I clarified. "It's fine. It's, uh, been fine for almost 30 years now."

"Well, it was thirty years before that that I last went through Panama," the man snapped. "So don't be all haughty. Say, those are nice wings on your chest. I never had a pair like that."

"When did…"

"I figured the ferry system couldn't be much use anymore. Everybody's got a car now so they've got to put bridges in because the roads go everywhere. Well, not everywhere," he looked around. "But most places. You know, I've lived without a car for forty years and it hasn't bothered me at all. I don't know why everybody has to have one. How do they afford them, first of all, and why can't they just walk?"

Luz looked around half expecting the people of the man's derision to come out of the forest.

"Who are…"

"Gave my last one to my first wife," the man continued. "God rest her soul. Bought one for my second wife but haven't had a need for it myself. The bus goes everywhere. Or gets me close. I wish the bus could get up here. If it did I never would have twisted my ankle. And folks call me Diego," he added before Walt could interrupt him again.

Walt relaxed when he said that. The man noticed.

"Do I know you?" he asked.

"No," Walt replied. "It's just that we work with a guy who's a bit of a nut. He goes on about some pilot being stuck down in the jungle and we thought you might be him."

"Well, I wasn't stuck until recently so I doubt it."

"You look familiar, though," Walt remarked. He walked through the flowers to look at the man from another angle. "Did you used to have a moustache? A big fluffy one?"

"Nope," the man replied. "Mine was short and thin. An Errol Flynn man, I was. You boys don't remember him but in the thirties and forties he and Clark Gable were the fellows who set fashion. We all had their moustaches then. I kept mine for a long time. Didn't shave it off until I turned sixty. Until then I thought it looked distinguished but after sixty it just looked silly." He rubbed a finger across his upper lip, remembering. "And my new wife said it tickled."

Walt jerked a thumb at the Trimotor.

"That's your plane?"

"I said it was."

"Did you ever fly it with a scarf? A long white one? And a leather helmet with goggles?"

"The first models had open cockpits, young man. What do you think we wore?" He chuckled and looked at me. "Your friend here looks like he's seen a ghost."

"He has dreams," I explained.

"So do I but they're not about moustaches."

"I can see you with a big fluffy one," Walt insisted.

"Well, you won't. Sorry to disappoint you, old chum. You may be thinking of Arnie."

"Who's Arnie?"

"My brother. He had a big moustache. I don't think he would have described it as fluffy, though. 'Full' would be a more manly term."

"Did he fly?"

"Did he fly... did Al Capone carry a gun? What a question. He would laugh in your face if he were here. Of course he flew. Did he ever! Arnie was the real pilot in the family. Flew in France with the 17th Aero Squadron, then barn-stormed his way through the Twenties. He was never any Roscoe Turner but he was well-known at the time. We flew mail together. I was Chicago-Dallas and he was out of St. Louis. For a while we were both in the air more than we were on the ground. By the time I started flying, though, he had been doing it for ten years so he was the expert. He never let me forget it, either." Diego smiled, remembering.

"Did he teach you?"

"To fly? No. He tried, though. Arnie never thought I knew what I was doing, never thought I took it seriously. I was always doing too many other things – especially after we came south. He would spend fifteen hours a day flying if he could while I was always wandering off to some museum, or to see some girl, or to tour some ruins. I liked to fly but there's more to life than that. I thought so, anyway. I told him we had to see the world while we could but all he could think about was getting up in the air. He was always lecturing me, always following me around, telling me how to do this or that. Looking out for me, he was – or trying to."

"Where is he now?" I asked.

"Oh, he died a long time ago. Back in '35 in a crash. About the only *bad* crash the Trimotors ever had."

"I'm sorry."

"I am, too. He had more looking out for me to do, and I always wanted to show him what he'd missed."

"I thought you said these were safe," Luz chided me, patting the nose of the Trimotor.

"They are," Diego answered testily. "But any plane will crash if you fly it into somebody else. That's what happened in Medellín. It was raining and Arnie was coming in to land while another fellow was taking off. They didn't see each other and collided about three hundred feet up. It happens. We didn't fly in weather if we could help it. Did a lot of scud-running, instead. The problem with scud-running, though, is that every pilot always seems to pick the same cloud to run under!"

"Things haven't changed," Walt remarked.

"No? Well, the real shame is that lots of folks died that day. It's bad enough for a pilot to kill himself but he's not supposed to hurt the passengers."

"How about your passengers?" Luz asked with typical loadmaster tact. He jabbed a thumb toward the Trimotor.

"They were fine," Diego snapped. "Not even a bloody nose when I put her down." After a minute, though, he felt obliged to add, "Don't get me wrong. I wrecked a couple of other times. There was one place in Missouri that I always seemed to have engine trouble over – one farmer there got so used to me landing in his field he wanted to charge me rent. And I balled up a Stearman towing a banner in '38. I was trying to impress my wife and caught the thing on a water tower. Damned near yanked me out of the air. Don't do that."

"Did you ever have to parachute out?" I asked.

"They didn't carry parachutes then," Walt corrected me.

"Who says?" Diego rejoined.

"I don't know. I thought...well, you know, back then it wasn't..."

"What?"

"It wasn't chivalrous, right? Carrying a parachute was a sign of cowardice."

Diego laughed. "What a load of crap! Everybody carried a parachute unless you were a blithering idiot. Hell, son, if all they'd give us was a giant goose-down pillow I would have carried that if I thought it would cushion my noggin in the fall. Chivalrous, my butt...where do you kids get these ideas?"

Diego limped around the lean-to to look at his plane, then laboriously worked himself into a seat on one of the open logs.

"You don't look like a Diego," Luz commented, taking a seat on the other log.

"No? You're a quick one, you are."

"What's your real name?"

"It's...what's that wire up there?" Diego interrupted himself, distracted.

"What? Where?"

"That long one on your plane. Going up to the tail."

"That's our HF antenna," I explained. "For a short-wave radio. It lets us talk all the way back to Panama when the weather's good."

"Hmph. Radios. We didn't carry them," he said, nodding to his Ford. "Electronic suggestion boxes, I call them. Nobody on the ground ever had anything useful to tell me. And in the air? Heck, if you gave some fellows radios they would jaw-jack at each other all the way down the mail line."

"That hasn't changed, either," I agreed with a glance at Walt.

"You have to have a radio on planes now," he replied, only a bit defensive.

"Maybe, but I stopped flying after the war so my experience is a little out of date. My guess is you fellows do all kinds of things on a plane that we never did. And except for my baby here I haven't seen another plane in I can't tell you how long."

He sat stiffly on the log with his bad leg cocked before him.

"How long have you been up here?"

"Three months," the old man said. "But I come up every year to check on my plane."

"From where?"

"Celendin."

"Where's that?"

"On the road to Cajamarca."

Cajamarca. I remembered an old lithograph in a history book showing the conquistadors fighting the Incas in that town's main square. The square where they killed Atahualpa and put his empire on the run.

"Cajamarca?" Walt repeated. "That's a long way from here."

"A very long way," the man agreed. "But the bus gets close. Then it's about a week's walk."

"A week?" Luz exclaimed. He gestured to the mountains, his eyes wide. "Over those?"

The old man grinned. He had great teeth.

"Fresh air is good for you, young fellow! Yes, over those. It's not as bad as it looks. You could do it in half the time, I'm sure, but I'm slow. It's quite walkable until you come down that wall. Then you really need to find the trail. I still have trouble. You would think after sixty years I would have the route nailed down but every year I wander around looking for landmarks. It's thick up there. There's rain and things grow fast."

"You've been coming here for sixty years?" I asked.

"Mm-hmm. Since I landed and had to walk out the first time. Makes me feel good."

"But...sixty years?"

"Goes by faster than you know it, sonny boy. Seems like yesterday that I was your age, flying around here without a care in the world."

"Did you ever hear of a guy named Jimmy Angel?"

Diego nodded. "Of course. You say "hear of him" like he was famous. He wasn't famous, he just flew around like the rest of us. Gold-digger, he was. That's what we called him. Half the time when someone hired him he never got to where he was going because he turned off somewhere looking for gold. Worthless as an employee. Good pilot, though. Crashed better than anybody I know."

Luz returned to the subject of hiking into the valley. He couldn't believe that's how Diego had gotten there and it was easy to share his doubt. We were in the middle of absolutely nowhere.

But if that was the reality, then reality didn't bother Diego. He found our disbelief amusing. So far he had not shown even a hint of disquiet about three Americans suddenly dropping into his idyllic retreat. That didn't change. The more we talked the more he warmed to us – or to having an audience, anyway. He must have been a pilot because one story led into another. When Luz asked him about fuel for the Trimotor he launched into a disquisition on load characteristics, segued into a discussion of his passengers the day he crashed, followed that with a story about the Cleveland Air Races, and ended up wondering aloud why no pilots wore seat belts until the 1930s.

"No seat belts?" Luz asked. "In an open cockpit? Wasn't that dangerous?"

"Course it was. Guys used to get bounced out all the time. Then we closed the cockpits and figured that was enough. If the damned government hadn't stepped in we never would have worn them. I never did like FDR and now I remember why."

"Wait a minute, wait a minute," Walt pleaded. "Can we back up a little? You landed here when? In 1930?"

"Yup. Right after Independence Day. That's Peru's Independence Day, not ours. I'd brought some people into Lima for the holiday and was taking them back to Cuzco when we picked up ice. Lost one engine and then blew a seal in another – we were riding it in and my last motor was just following us to the crash. I was sure I was going to die. We descended into clouds and I didn't figure they would open up again before I hit something. But then they did and I caught sight of this valley." He turned in his seat and pointed out across the expanse of gentians. "I've loved it here ever since. How can you not? That day when the window cleared and I saw these flowers it was like somebody saying, 'Here, you can have life again. Come on down.' But I always thought I would fly back out."

Walt and Luz and I exchanged glances. This guy made an emergency landing when Hoover was president and was still around to tell us about it?

"C'mon, don't look so shocked, you nitwits. You make me feel old when you get those weepie looks on your faces. Yes, it was sixty years ago but that's not so long, you know. Ask your dad. And believe it or not, it wasn't as far a walk back then to get out of here. There used to be a village eight miles west of here at the bottom of the mountains. It only disappeared in the 1960s when everyone moved into towns. Until we walked there – and we *all* walked there," he added with a glance at Luz, "even the women – the company thought we were dead. Hell, ten years later I was still running into people who thought I had packed it in that day. I suppose I should have. But I didn't. That's the way it goes."

"But if it was sixty years ago why do you still come up here? I mean, there are other planes..."

"Sure, and I flew them. I even left Peru for a while. Flew anything with a prop, anywhere there was a job. Then Arnie and I went to Bogotá and flew Trimotors there. You know the national airline, Avianca? Well, it used to be two companies, SACO and SCADTA. SCADTA was a German company and Arnie knew a guy there who he flew against in the war. That's the guy that flew into him. How's that for destiny, hey? Anyway, for a few years I left my goose..."

"You left what?"

"My goose. The Fords were called Tin Gooses, or Tin Geese I guess. This is my Goose. Anyway, I didn't forget about her but just left her. Then I stopped flying for a while. It was hard to go up again after Arnie's accident. He'd always been there keeping an eye on me and I felt empty knowing he wasn't somewhere in the sky with me when I flew, so I walked away and did other things. That's probably why people thought I was dead. When I started up again I remembered this bird, thought I might come back, fix the engine, and fly her out. It took a while to find her again but I did. Cleaned her up, cleared a space... I fixed the engine soon enough but after that it was one thing after another. You boys might know that the weather in this area is usually right down to the ground. It doesn't rain hard but even in the summer it's almost always wet. Half the time the ground is too soft even to taxi. I need a dry week just to get the plane moving and then a clear day to get out of here because my instruments aren't worth beans."

"But does this plane have the power...?" "Of course it has the power. You think I would have flown up this way in the first place if I didn't have the power? But I just told you: when I happened to be here *and* the weather was good, it was one thing after another. Another engine crapped out or I had a flat tire or oil pissed all over. Came up one year and found hail had darn near beaten my baby to death. That's when I built the shelter. Another time I taxied out and went right into a hole. Over where you fellows came in. You can thank me for filling it, by the way. Broke a strut that time. It was always something. The tires were the hardest to fix. And other things happened. There was the war, and then some fighting here in Peru that made it hard to travel. It took longer and longer but I couldn't give her up. I suppose at some point I got too old but you know, I always saw myself flying out of here one day. I have dreams, too," he smiled at Walt. "So I kept coming back. I don't know where the time has gone."

"Why didn't you get help?" Luz asked.

"I did, genius. Just because I'm old doesn't mean I'm stupid." He leaned from his log and studied Luz's uniform. "What's your job, anyway? You have different wings."

"I'm a loadmaster."

"What's that?"

"I, uh, load the plane," Luz replied.

"What do you mean, you load the plane?"

"I load the plane," Luz repeated. "These guys fly, but I put everything on board and tie it down."

Diego stared, waiting for the punch line. When Luz kept quiet he said, "Oh, come on. What do you really do?"

"That's what I do," Luz insisted.

Diego looked at me and then at Walt. "You have somebody load the plane for you? What are you, a couple of pansies? Is he serious?"

"He's serious," Walt said. "It's complicated. We have a lot to do before flights and..."

"Complicated?" the old man barked. "You put stuff in the back, boy, and take off. How complicated is that? I never needed a loadmaster. What kind of silly job is that?"

"Um, you were about to say how you had people come up here with you?" I suggested before Luz grew angry.

Diego rolled his eyes, glanced once more at Luz and chuckled, but agreed to change the subject.

"Yes, people have come up with me over the years. Hell, I've overhauled all those engines more than once. But after a while folks move on to other things. After ten years of failure, it got hard to get anyone to come. After twenty years, it got *really* hard. And I admit, there were years when I didn't get up here myself. I had jobs to do. My boy came up with me the most but he's getting on in years and doesn't walk as much as he used to."

"How old is he?" I asked.

"Seventy-four."

"Seventy-four! How old are you?"

"Ninety-two."

"What?!"

You could have knocked me over with a wind sock. The man didn't look a day over seventy. More than that, the idea of someone in his nineties walking alone into the Andes was preposterous.

"I always wanted to fly out of here," the man continued, relishing our shock, "but have come to accept that maybe this is where my old goose is meant to stay. To tell the truth, until you flew overhead I thought I was going to join her."

"What do you mean?" Luz asked, finding words.

The man took a crutch and pointed it at his foot.

"I twisted this bad coming down the trail three months ago. Twisted my ankle – what a stupid thing to do! You would think a snake or a jaguar would get me. Hell, at ninety-two you would think I would just fall over with a coronary. But no. Anyway, not a problem. I don't heal the way I used to but figured I would be alright. I got trapped here once back in the forties and have stocked up food since so I could take time to let it heal. But then I twisted the damned thing again trying to leave before it was ready. Ooo, that one hurt! I had to crawl my way back to the cabin." He waved toward the forest. Now that we knew where to look we could make out a small building inside the tree line. "After that I found out I should have stocked up more. Wasn't planning on relocating if you know what I mean."

"Don't you have a radio or something?" I asked.

"No."

"But wouldn't someone look for you? Your son, maybe?"

The old man smiled. "I have a history of disappearing. About Christmas someone might get worried but before then, not likely. Arnie used to throw a fit if I went off exploring without telling him. But then, he used to do the same thing in his plane. He would take off and be gone for weeks and then come back with stories of Tierra del Fuego or the coast of Brazil. It's a family trait. Doones have always been rovers."

Walt nearly coughed up a lung.

"What did you say?" he croaked. "Your name is Doone?"

"What of it? I'm as Irish as Paddy's pig."

"But you said your name was Diego."

The old man shook his head. "No, I said folks *call* me Diego. That's because around here they have trouble with the L. Besides, as your loadmaster noted I don't look like a Diego, do I? You should have figured out on your own that I'm not from Tijuana."

Walt rubbed his face in his hands. He kept his eyes covered as though hoping to wake up back in his bed. Luz crossed himself and muttered a prayer in Spanish.

"You're Diegel Doone," I said when I overcame my own shock.

"At your service. Though it's been a long time since I've heard someone else say that name! What's wrong? Am I in trouble? Some copper still have a warrant out on me? Heh-heh. You boys look like you've seen a ghost. I'm no ghost!" he laughed, and rapped his knuckles against his head. "Not yet!"

Walt dropped his hands and sat down in the flowers, disappearing up to his face. It took him a while to look up and meet the eyes of the man who everyone but Skinny Steve thought was a myth.

***

We sat for a while. It was a measure of the quiet that when a breeze stirred the flowers we heard them shiver. Diego reached up and caressed a blade of the nose prop.

"The snows will start soon," he picked up again. "There's water in the creek and fish, too, but – heh, heh – I'm ninety-two. I've caught a few but mostly those fish just laugh their behinds off watching me try to put them into a pan. I was starting to think I would have to hang it up for good. Then you boys flew over. How's that for coincidence, hey?"

Walt frowned. "You twisted your ankle when?" he asked.

"Oh, what...ten, twelve weeks ago?" Diego said. "I told you, I heal slow."

"But I dreamed about you over a year ago!"

"Whoa there, fellow! If you're dreaming about me you're a confused young man."

"No, no. You're missing the point. It's a long story."

"And you'd better start telling it, Walt," I broke in. "You need to explain your screwy life. You...wait a minute. Hey, sir, are you hungry?"

Diego didn't bother to make a joke of his answer. "Yes, I am."

Luz jumped to his feet. "I'll get it. I've got all kinds of stuff in the hell-hole."

"Thanks, Luz."

He brought Diego a sandwich from Ari's Burger, some water, and a bottle of Inca cola. Diego went for the cola first and then after a brief study of the sandwich wolfed that down, too. If I expected a man in his tenth decade to be more picky about his food I was wrong. He ate like a ravenous teenager.

"Thank you, Mr. *Load*master," he said, and smiled at Luz. "I'll be kinder about your profession from now on, I promise. Now, son," he turned to Walt. "You said something about me prancing through your dreams. What's all that about?"

Walt plucked a gentian to chew on and began his tale.

***

I have a friend who once flew rescue helicopters in Alaska. One night he and his copilot took off in a blizzard to find a stranded fishing boat with a sick captain. They followed the coast toward Kenai but soon lost the horizon so they turned inland to avoid the snow. It didn't work. A white-out ensued. The flakes fell fat and fast, filling their windscreen. They became lost. They couldn't climb for fear of icing; they couldn't land because they couldn't see the ground. All they could do was stay level, watch their altimeter, and pray they didn't hit anything.

Suddenly lights appeared. It was an airstrip, a runway in the middle of nowhere, two rows of white and red lights stretching into the night like a divine railroad. A local, an old Inuit man with a Super Cub, had heard them circling in the night and figured they were in trouble so he went outside and turned on the lights of his private strip. They lined up on the vision and rolled their helicopter onto the packed snow, praising their luck and thanking the man profusely for saving their lives.

They stayed until the storm passed, huddled by the window, watching the snow fall. The Inuit was a sphinx. He puffed a pipe and regarded them doubtfully through the smoke, clearly thinking they were crazy for being out in such weather. But he held his tongue. Only when they discussed their anxiety over finding the boat did he offer advice: "Follow the caribou," he rumbled. Huh? my friend asked. "Follow the caribou," the man repeated.

They thought the old man was on drugs. They took off, tried to find their way out of the mountains, and became lost again. Just when they were ready to give up hope a dark line appeared on the white tableau: a wide swathe of caribou tracks. The herd's trail led into a canyon and down to the coast, opening onto a wide plain that ended in a cove where the sick captain waited. He had thought they would never come.

***

When Walt finished his story Diego said nothing about caribou but he regarded us for a long time with the same ancient and untroubled expression that I imagined on the old Inuit's face. He sat quietly, hunched over with his crutches crossed on his lap. I thought he had gone to sleep.

After a while he lifted his head.

"Funny things, dreams," he nodded. "Let's see that airplane of yours."

We helped him to his feet. Luz went ahead of us and started the APU, then opened the cargo door and lowered the ramp so it would be easier for Diego to go on board. The ramp dropped into the flowers where the long furrows from our landing roll met the plane. They looked like little roads, three deep paths leading from the horizon right into the cabin.

"Well, I'll be," Diego said, looking inside. With help he hobbled up the ramp.

Walt gave him the tour, starting from the back and laying out everything a pilot would want to know just as Bob Harcourt had done for me the first time I stepped aboard a C-27. Diego devoured every word as hungrily as he had eaten Luz's sandwich. His eyes were bright, his mouth open. He asked questions but mostly just said "oh." Again and again it was "oh," so overcome with emotion was he that nothing would follow. He reached out and touched whatever Walt pointed to.

"And up here's the cockpit," Walt told him. "Don't bother to climb the stair with your foot but you can see it from here..."

"Yes, I can."

Diego leaned over the steps and surveyed the cockpit, his eyes scanning the panel the way a good carpenter might survey another craftsman's tools. Through the front window the Trimotor poked its nose around the side of the hill and eyed the C-27 from the other direction.

"You can go up if you'd like," Walt offered.

"No," was the reply. "Not yet."

I cleared my throat. Getting Walt's attention, I motioned him to the back of the cabin.

"What are we going to do?" I whispered.

"Take him out of here. What else?"

"As simple as that? What if he doesn't want to go?"

"He'll go. He'll starve if he doesn't."

"He's attached to that plane."

"Planes don't eat. We'll take him to Lima. We can drop him off and have the station manager make sure he gets on a bus to Cajamarca."

"And if he says no?"

Walt held up his hands.

"Mike, what do you want me to do? Look, I agree this valley is just like Evan described but I don't know what to do about it. There's no gold, there's no Incas, there's no treasure or clues or arrows pointing the way to somewhere else. There's just a senile old man who has a lot of stories and nothing to do with my dream. And there's no way he's been coming here for sixty years," he hissed. "That's ludicrous. I don't know how he got up here but he didn't walk and there's no way he's ninety years old. My grandpa doesn't look that good and he just turned sixty."

Diego turned from the cockpit steps. "It's getting late," he said and hobbled past us toward the ramp. "You boys will want to get out of here while there's still light."

"About that," Walt followed him. "Listen, sir, we're heading down to the capital. We don't have time or a clearance to go into Cajamarca but why don't you come with us to Lima? We can get you on a bus there that'll take you home."

Diego allowed Luz to help him down the ramp. For a fellow who didn't think much of loadmasters he was finding ours a real convenience. On the ground he spoke as though he hadn't heard Walt.

"These fellas can get your plane ready to go," he said. "Why don't you come with me real quick? I've got something I want to show you."

Walt hesitated. "What is it?"

"Something you might be interested in. Come on, come on."

With a glance toward me and Luz, Walt followed Diego to the trees.

***

Taking off from a high-altitude field is an exercise in faith. It can take so much longer to reach your speeds that often on the long takeoff roll pilots find themselves staring at the instruments and wondering why physics won't cooperate. Trying to accelerate in a field of waist-high plants promised to be even more of a challenge. I looked down the valley behind our plane and wondered – much too late – if the Chuck was up to the task.

"Luz, I'm going for a walk," I called.

"Roger, sir. I'm ready when you guys are."

I walked up the tracks of our landing roll to where we had first touched down, stopping to muse on the first flower that was struck by our gear. If flowers could think, what must that one have thought as it watched fifty thousand tons of metal appear in the sky and head straight for it? And how about the flower next to it that still stood straight and tall? Probably *Why me?* and *Sucks to be you,* in that order.

Our landing roll was two thousand feet. I continued up the valley that distance again, watching the ground and crushing as many flowers underfoot as I could to mark the way. I also picked a bunch and shoved them in my pockets – Billie wasn't the flowers type but she was still a woman, and nobody had ever given her gentians.

There was nothing to note about the surface: no rocks, no holes, no dips. If Nature wanted to keep us in, she wouldn't do it with the valley floor. I looked up to the valley walls. *But she might do it with those...*

Back at the plane I ran through our performance data. At this altitude it wasn't great. And since the overcast layer had settled down once more onto the top of the mountain, once we cleared the valley we wouldn't be able to see the terrain around us any better than we had coming in. I tried to remember our path leading to the gentians – we had zig-zagged so much looking for a place to drop the ashes that I didn't remember where or how exactly we had approached the valley.

When Walt and Diegel returned to the plane, Walt no longer looked nervous. He carried a canvas backpack and whistled as he hopped up the steps.

"Mike, buddy, I need a favor," he said, jumping up to the cockpit.

"You're all chipper. What's he got back there? A pile of gold?"

"Not a thing," he said with a shake of his head. "Nothing but four walls and a roof. It's a loadmaster retirement home."

"Then what are you all happy about?"

"Because we're done," he said simply. "The search is over. We've got Number 27 and he's right here, walking on a pair of crutches." He pointed outside to Diegel, who continued around back to the ramp.

"Glad to hear it," I said, holding up my own numbers that I had computed for our climb rate. "You can explain it to me later. In the meantime, let's talk about the departure out of here. It's going to be hairy."

"Not worried about it," he said.

"Well, I am. We'll need to hold best angle in the climb regardless of direction but that still won't guarantee terrain clearance." I ran him through the data and then held up the map. "Maybe you haven't noticed but our charts aren't exactly precise in this section of the Andes."

"Not a problem," he insisted. "We've got a ringer on board who knows these mountains inside and out. And that's the favor I need. We've got a new member of the crew who wants to fly this leg."

"Huh?"

Diegel popped his head into the cockpit.

"Come on, sonny boy, don't be a stick hog! I haven't flown in forty-four years and it's time I did. Move over!"

"Walt, are you serious?" We had already broken half a dozen regulations since breakfast but putting someone at the controls who was unqualified in the plane was a big one. It wasn't a matter of safety: we could have put a giraffe in the copilot's seat and I would have trusted Walt to keep control of the plane. Still, this was a new one for me.

Walt climbed over the center panel and sat sideways in his seat.

"Mike, I know this is unusual but look around. For eighteen months I've dragged my ass all over this continent – as have you, by the way – in search of a bunch of junk that doesn't make sense to any of us. And all of it brought us right here, today, to this valley. We're sitting here because some old guy in a dream pointed us this way and darn it, we're done. It's over. The list is complete and I'm going home and going to bed and the only thing I'm going to dream about from now on is naked women and a job at Delta."

"I'm happy for you."

"But there's one more dream out there and it's standing right in front of you." He pointed to Diegel who grinned and knocked his knuckles against his head in response. "This fine young postal aviator has been waiting sixty years to fly out of this valley and today he's going to do it!"

I looked at the splint on Diegel's leg.

"Can you fly?" I asked.

He misunderstood me. "Don't worry about me, young man. Don't think of how long it's been since I've flown. Think of how long it's been since I've crashed! That's 45 years! You should hope to beat that record. Now get out of my seat."

***

From the third seat, all I saw out the front window was flowers. The C-27 rumbled softly as Walt turned it around and lined up on our landing roll. Luz strapped himself into the fold-down seat by the door but not before hitting me on the shoulder.

"Don't let them hit a mountain," he beseeched me. "If that old man doesn't know what he's doing, drag his ass out of the seat and I'll tie him down back here."

"I heard that!" Diegel shouted from up front. "It won't happen – but if it does, at least you'll have something to do!"

Walt walked Diegel through the take-off procedures and talked about the plane's handling. "It's a tough bird and there's a lot of wing out there," he instructed, "but at this altitude we have to keep the speed up or it won't fly. 101 is our magic number to get airborne. Then 120 to climb. Hold 120. Above that we'll climb slower. Below it we'll stall."

"Let's not stall," Luz muttered over the intercom.

Diegel ignored him. "Which way were you thinking of going?" he asked.

"Uhhhh," said Walt. "Well, we came in from the east."

"Nope," said Diegel. "You go that way, you'll have a hellacious tailwind that'll push you into a mountain before you can climb out of it. Even if you don't hit something you'll just have to come back the same way."

"Okay, then how about south? We were working our way along the ridge when we stumbled on this place, so..."

"So you're going to try scud-running with clouds that have come down at least 400 feet since you landed? Boy, where did you get your license?"

Walt bit his tongue.

"What would you suggest, sir?" he asked.

"Ooo, *sir*. Aren't we formal? But keep it up, I like it. Okay, look: there's a phenomenon across this part of the cordillera where the wind screams through but never gets too high. It puts a cap of clouds over the peaks for about 5,000 feet and sometimes higher, and then comes down and cracks like a whip over the jungle..."

"They call it 'mountain wave' now," I interjected.

"Bully for them," Diegel snapped. "You can't fly with it. Well, you can, I suppose, but it'll be like running rapids in an inner tube. And there's no guarantee it won't throw you into the ground instead of washing you over it. So you can't go east. But you can't go north or south, either, because you still have to climb through it and you don't want to do that broadside on. That will be one bumpy ride you'll never forget – trust me, I went through it on the way in here."

"That was sixty years ago."

"Weather doesn't change, sonny."

"So let me guess," Walt proposed. "We'll go west."

Diegel touched his nose and pointed at Walt like he was the bright pupil.

"Ah, okay," I spoke up. "But one thing we *do* know from the map is that our highest terrain is still to the west. We're only in the foothills here, remember: we haven't yet crossed the main spine of the Andes."

"That's right."

"And we'll be flying into a headwind," I continued. "Which means we'll still be surfing those rapids you mentioned, *sir*, except now we'll be doing it upstream." I added carefully, "That doesn't sound smart."

Diegel guffawed. "Smart? Smart? You fellows just landed in a mountain meadow because you wanted to site-see. Don't tell me about smart." He cocked his left foot so it would fit between the rudder pedals and scooted his seat forward a notch. "Now look. Here's what I suggest – and keep in mind I've only got sixty years of hiking around these mountains so maybe my knowledge isn't quite as up to speed as that map you've got. That wind shear overhead is there 90% of the time, so unless you want to set here and wait a couple of months for a clear day this is what we're going to have to do. We take off, spiral if we have to to get our speed and our altitude, and then turn straight west into the wind and climb like a rocket ship until we get through it. Sure, it might be bumpy, but we used to use that 'mountain wave' of yours all the time to get over the hills whenever we were low on power. If I can do it in a Trimotor, you can do it in this thing. You don't cross the ground fast but that's okay – you're in no hurry. So long as you're climbing all the time, that's what you care about. And so long as you don't lose an engine, that is, but you boys seem to have confidence in your machine here."

"We won't lose an engine," Walt assured him.

"Then you have nothing to worry about," Diegel replied.

Walt chewed his lower lip, thinking. When he looked my way, I signaled that I didn't have any better ideas.

"Luz?" he asked. "Any input?"

"I heard the word turbulence," Luz responded. "So I'm going to tighten my seatbelt and pray to the Virgin Mary."

Diegel slapped the dash in approval. "It never hurts," he exclaimed.

"Okay, then," Walt said. He adjusted his own seat. "Then let's do it."

"Whoa, whoa, whoa," Diegel stopped him. "Are we going now?"

"Yeah. If you're ready, that is."

Diegel sat up straight and rubbed his chin. "Just give me a minute," he requested. "Please, if you would. Just give me a minute."

We sat there then, the three of us in the cockpit, without speaking. Diegel gazed out the front window, then the side, and then even the overhead where he pushed the curtain out of the way. With help from me he popped open the side window and stuck his head out, breathing in the sweet fragrance of the gentians for one more blast of clean, ageless air into his lungs. But mostly he sat with his hands on the controls, surveying the instrument panel and peering over the dash at the ocean of blue and the green wall of the valley miles away.

"I always knew I would fly out of this valley," he said quietly. "I didn't know how but I knew I would. It seems like only last week that we landed. I remember rolling through these flowers, throwing them every which way, and thinking about how I would turn around and get right back out. I thought it would be in my Goose. Then for years I pictured myself back in the cockpit, looking over the nose and trying to keep her straight on the takeoff roll. But the cockpit didn't always look the same. Now I understand why." He gripped the controls with his right hand and rested his left on the throttles.

"Then let's get you back up in the air," Walt urged. "You have the aircraft. I'll steer and help you on that left rudder, but it's all you from here on out. Show us how to fly the mail."

Diegel pushed up the throttles. The C-27 sat still, making noise but not going anywhere. Only when he got the engines above 600 foot-pounds did we lurch forward an inch. Then another. Finally, at 800 on the torque gauges the Mighty Chuck rolled forward and never looked back. I pulled my eyes away from the gauges long enough to check on Diegel and saw in his face the picture of concentration, the visage of a man feeling every piece of the plane. He also looked happy.

Walt kept the nose pointed down the center row that we had carved earlier. We rolled through 2,000 feet, then 3,000. The airspeed indicator got to 90 knots and then stagnated. Worried that we were driving so long, I was about to suggest to Walt that maybe it was clogged when suddenly the needle jumped and popped over the 100 mark.

"Rotate," Walt called.

Diegel squeezed back on the controls and we flew into the air.

"Yeah, baby!" Luz called from the back as the bumping stopped and the cabin quit shaking like a paint mixer. "That's what I like!"

Diegel's eyes widened and so did his smile. He let the C-27 cruise over the gentians like an eagle skimming a lake. Our airspeed climbed to 110 but he held us in ground effect until it gained another ten knots. Then the nose came up and we banked gently to the right. "I'll come right and then back to the left," he advised.

"Alright," said Walt. He was rarely so laconic. That more than anything told me he was concentrating, too.

Diegel took us to the right wall of the valley, still in calm winds, and then reversed course to face directly at the other side. Not satisfied with the picture, he reversed course again and flew a racetrack to get comfortable. He kept the nose up as the C-27 accelerated, holding the speed right on 120 as Walt had instructed. Walt raised the gear. Our climb rate reached 500 feet per minute, then 700, then 900. Facing west again, Diegel found the spot on the wall he was looking for. We shot above the valley rim and into the cloud deck. In seconds the gentians were lost to view.

"There we are, just as advertised," Diegel commented, his eyes glued to the panel now that everything outside turned white. He referred to the turbulence which started as soon as we went into the clouds. Now instead of bouncing up and down we rocked like a ship plowing high seas. "But don't worry, look what it's doing to our climb rate."

The needle on the vertical velocity indicator jumped from below 1,000 feet per minute to over 2,000. Our speed stayed rock-steady on 120 KIAS.

"Are we supposed to shake this much?" Luz asked, concern in his voice. The broom popped out of its bracket on the wall and fell onto the fold-down seats. Something in the latrine fell over.

"It's all good, Load," Walt assured him, his voice shaking as he bounced in his seat. "Our speed's good and we're climbing. We should get out of it soon."

I studied our radar screen. Because our nose was so high we had the angle pointed down to see if it would pick up any terrain. There was one red blip off to our right but nothing straight ahead. Above the radar was our groundspeed readout as measured by the inertial system. It read 62. That meant the wind in our face was a good 60 miles per hour strong. We were flying into a baby jet stream.

"Whoo-hoo!" cried Diegel as a gust from that stream picked us up and then pushed us back down, making everyone light in their seats. "Hee-hee. *That's* a feeling that hasn't changed!"

We passed 15,000 feet, then 16,000, still in cloud. For a guy who hadn't flown in nearly fifty years, Diegel handled the instrument conditions really well. He gripped the yoke with both hands and hunched over it to focus on the artificial horizon, looking like nothing so much as granny behind the wheel, but it worked. Except for the turbulence the needle on the airspeed indicator never budged from 120. The guy knew what he was doing.

At 17,500 feet we broke into the clear. The clouds dropped away and we found ourselves suddenly in crystalline air with nothing but the sky above and clouds and snow below. To our left and right – at our altitude – were mountain peaks. We had threaded one of the few gaps in the chain for as far as we could see.

"Oh my," Diegel exclaimed. "Oh my, that's beautiful."

Walt let him nose over and accelerate. They raised the flaps and finished the After Takeoff checks, then Walt computed a course for Lima.

"That was a great job for someone who hasn't flown in almost half a century," he complimented Diegel.

"Oh, come on, son. That was a good job even for someone who flew yesterday."

"Ha, ha! You must be a pilot with that ego. Well, good on you. You still have the skills."

"I do, don't I?" Declan agreed. "Yes, sir, I think I do." He started to say something else but his attention was stolen by the view outside. The Andes were beneath. The air was of a clarity unheard of at sea-level and our vantage point gave us a god's-eye view of some of the highest terrain on earth.

Diegel stared out the window in satisfaction. "Do you see that, boys? Do you see that view? My goodness, look at those mountains. It's been so long...it's been so long...damn, Arnie, they haven't changed...you were right...there's nothing like it..."

"Are you okay?" Walt asked, "Do you want me to take it?"

Diegel answered without turning. "Are you kidding?"

"Don't give it to him, Diegel," I warned. "Walt's the original stick-hog. If you give up the controls you'll never get them back."

He snapped out of his reverie. "Then I'll just hang onto them, if you don't mind," he chuckled. "No, no. I'm not used to having company in the cockpit. Hell, I'm not even used to being *in* a cockpit anymore. You boys speak up when you want to fly but otherwise... well, it feels good to have a plane again."

"Keep it, keep it," Walt insisted. "We've got, oh, one-plus-ten of fuel to play with. In fact, we're over the highest stuff now so the ground should start to drop soon – now that we can see, if you want to maneuver some on the way down it's all you."

"Are you serious?"

"Absolutely. Lima's that way a hundred and forty miles. So long as you get us there before dark and before we run out of gas, this leg is all yours. Come on, you say you've been tramping these mountains for decades – show us what you know."

Diegel's eyes shone. His hands gripped the controls like he was afraid they would run away. I knew what he was feeling. My first flight was only four years in the past, the flight where I had had to pay my instructor a ceremonial dollar for the privilege of getting me airborne. I still remembered what it was like to feel a plane rumble beneath me and to know I controlled what it did. Like any other that experience dulled with time but Diegel now was feeling it fresh. At ninety-two years old he was getting to feel like he was on a dollar ride all over again.

"Alrighty," he said. "Okay. Let's just bring it down a bit, then. See that peak? On the other side of it is one of the highest cities in the world. It's a miserable place, wicked cold, but there's a *parillada* there where you can get great steak and boiled potatoes. Then we can go south and down to the national park. There's a village there outside of Huánuco where I've been transferring buses for years...if you fellows will indulge me I'd like to give it a little buzz..."

As we cleared the spine of the cordillera, he pulled power and started a descent. The look on his face was priceless.

7

Fin

Walt and I flew up to Changuinola a month later. It was a beautiful day in the middle of rainy season, where white clouds floated at all altitudes and the occasional dark one gave them perspective. We were both in a good mood, me because I had just learned that the Air Force would allow me to extend my assignment in Panama for another year, and Walt because...well, because he was flying.

He had relaxed since our flight with Diegel Doone. Now that the search was over, in fact, Walt looked ten years younger. He could sleep again and he stopped heading to the flight line each day with a checklist of things he felt obliged to get done. Maybe neither one of us could hike to the top of the Andes but we could fly again just for the fun of it.

"You know, I never asked you what you saw in his cabin," I said as the Caribbean Ocean appeared off our right wing.

"Hmm?"

"You didn't think he was who he said he was," I reminded him. "Then you went to his cabin and came back a believer. What did he have there that convinced you?"

Walt nodded. "A picture of his brother. From a newspaper."

"And let me guess…"

"Uh-huh. He was right out of my dream."

We flew for a while in silence.

"Did you see the message from Georgie?" he asked. "The station manager in Lima?"

"No. He wreck another car?"

"No, it was about Diegel."

"Oh, no. He didn't die, did he?"

"Not hardly. He sent a note to Georgie asking him to get hold of your friend Harry. Since you suggested it, Diegel's excited about getting back up to his Goose first thing in the spring. He wants to get on Harry's calendar."

"I've already talked to Harry. He heard the word Trimotor and started drooling. He's ready to go. He might even get in shape for the hike."

"He may not have to. Georgie said Diegel's already made arrangements with a flight school in Lima to get his license re-current. He starts in January."

"At ninety-two years old?"

Walt grinned. "Ninety-three by then. And whoever his instructor is, he had better be on the ball. That old man will fly rings around him."

***

We carried three pallets of construction gear for some engineers working in the national park west of Changuinola. After dropping them off we returned to Howard to pick up a small boat that they would use as well. We also picked up the Pinheads, Jake, Kurt, and Lowell.

It was the start of a long weekend and they were going to Bocas del Toro to scuba dive.

On each trip we cruised northwest to the coast and then west toward Costa Rica until reaching Changuinola. The route took us over the best parts of Bocas del Toro Province: the Bocas archipelago, the Changuinola Canal, and the vast acres of banana plantations that surrounded our destination. The last thirty miles in particular was a matchless buffet of colors glistening in the coastal heat. Its kaleidoscope of hues prompted Walt to speak.

"I've been thinking, Mike," he said.

"Uh-oh."

"I know. I shouldn't, but...well, you're not going to like what I have to say."

"Then don't say it."

"Let me ask you this first: what did you think of Doone?"

"What do you mean, what did I think of him?"

"What did you think of him?"

I knew what I thought and knew it was the same that Walt thought: I accepted that Doone himself was the long-lived 'gold' we had been looking for and that the entire treasure hunt was an elaborate way for us to appreciate him once we found him. Beyond that, I tried not to think about it and said as much.

"Exactly," Walt proclaimed. "That's why I like flying with you, because we're on the same wavelength."

"We are NOT on the same wavelength," I assured him. "I don't have dreams. I sleep quite well, thank you, and when I fly it's to look at pretty clouds and to impress women. There's no more purpose to it than that."

Walt jabbed a finger into the air. "Ah! That segues neatly into what I want to tell you."

A mile below Almirante passed us by. A goliath ship with a banana painted on its hull was just pulling away from the pier. Almirante was the intergalactic center of banana exports.

"You're going into the banana business?" Clunk asked behind us, turning away from his magazine.

"No," Walt retorted. "Worse." He paused dramatically. "I've had another dream."

The response was immediate. A chorus of groans rose from everybody in the back who was on intercom, and while I said "no, no, no," Clunk looked around for something heavy to hit his pilot with.

"Now, hear me out..." Walt pleaded.

"We heard you out once before," Kurt cut him off. "That cost us a year and a half of looking for junk that sane people don't even keep in their garage. Lowell almost got eaten, TJ dropped that stele on his foot, and I was arrested in Suriname. Mike here almost crashed half a dozen times. You mention a dream again and we'll take you diving with us – except you won't get a tank."

"Hear, hear," agreed his companions.

"But..."

I laughed at him. "Do you really think anyone's going to listen to you, Walt? Hey, it was a great idea, I'll give you that. We all saw things we never would have seen otherwise. We all learned a lot about the locals and yes, there was some good flying. But forget it: we're not looking for anything else. We're not stealing any more relics from museums. What you've got, you've got, and you're not getting any more. It's over. The end. In Spanish, *el fin*."

"Yes!" he agreed. "You're absolutely right! It is the end. And I don't get anything else. Trust me, I don't *want* anything else. But ask yourself this, all of you: now that we've got all these things, all these 27 items from everywhere we've been, what do we do with them?"

There was silence. Though at first we had all thought that the items had some intrinsic meaning, by the end we saw them as a journey, not a destination. The idea now that there was anything to *do* with a stele, a stuffed coatamundi, or a skull was not something we thought about. Behind me Clunk scratched his head.

"Exactly," Walt said into the silence. "That's my problem, too. I didn't think about it right away because I was too focused on getting all of them together. But now that I've got this collection sitting in my house, it's been bugging me. What should we do with it? And then two weeks ago I woke up and had the answer."

"Shark 19, are you requesting to land?" The controller in Changuinola had picked us up with his binoculars. There was no one else in the sky.

"Sí, señor. Shark 19, request a straight-in to the northeast runway."

"Shark 19, you are cleared to land. Please hurry." The man wanted to go home for the day.

Walt pulled power and began a descent, taking us on a long final over the canal, the banana fields, and the Río Teribe where it flowed out of the national park and into the marshlands lining the coast. The ground rose on our left to form the Talamancas, a mountain chain that ran across the border and met up with the volcanoes of Costa Rica. On our right were the wetlands with their crazy-dangerous boardwalk, and on the far side of it the beach where countless turtles surfaced every year to lay their eggs.

On the ground we unloaded the boat. The guys grabbed their scuba gear and prepared to go. They would find a taxi to Almirante and then a ferry to Bocas del Toro. Lowell slung his bag over his shoulder and turned to Walt.

"You know, I'm a moron for asking," he said. "But we'll need something to laugh over beer tonight. So tell us: what's your grand plan for all that crap?"

Walt stood at the top of the ramp and held out his hands. "You tell me," he said. "It's so obvious: we've got all this stuff, it makes no sense to keep it, what do you think we should do with it?"

He was met with blank stares. It was so hard being a visionary.

"Alright," he said. "I'll tell you: we put it back."

Silence.

Finally, Flutie said, "Huh?"

"We put it back," Walt repeated. "The whole point of this hunt was to get us out of our shells, to give us purpose so we didn't just fly around the theater picking up pallets here and taking people there. Diegel and his brother spent years in the air and on the ground and they never saw half the things they wanted to see. But they watched other people go about their business and miss it all. They didn't want us to do that. So we went out on a giant treasure hunt and just think of everything we did! Think of everywhere we went that the Air Force was never going to send us! And now, it should all go back. We can't keep these things. They need to go back where they belong, to the people who gave them to us. They're treasures of this world, not ours. We'll just keep the memories."

"Put it back?" Evan asked.

"Yes!" said Walt.

The Pinheads looked at each other. Kurt shuffled his feet. Lowell fingered the scar on his leg.

Then Jake grabbed his backpack. "Yeah, have fun with that," he said. "I'm going diving."

"Damned straight."

"Hear, hear."

"I need a beer."

They drifted off toward the terminal, a low building with no sign and only one car parked in front of it. Walt and I were left alone. He watched them go.

"Okay!" he shouted after them. "You guys think about it! I've got all the stuff at my house so you know where it is! I'll just make a new list and we can...we can draw lots. Yeah, we'll draw lots and everybody can have a chance! Don't you worry about the schedule – I'll take care of that!"

In the distance, Tommy waved without turning around. They disappeared into a grove of palm trees lining the road to the terminal.

It was quiet on the field. Clunk sat at the bottom of the ramp folding tie-down straps.

"They seemed pretty enthusiastic," he said dryly.

Walt frowned but it took only a moment for his optimism to re-assert itself. "They'll come around," he promised. "I have a plan. It makes perfect sense. They'll come around, you'll see." He sighed and looked around the ramp as though trying to remember what we were doing there. From the cockpit came the low chatter of the radio where the tower controller was begging us to take-off. "Alright, then. I guess we're done for the day. You guys ready to fly home?"

"Absolutely."

"Then let's get moving. Button her up, Clunk." He held up a hand up to block the sun. "What do you say, Mike? It's Friday afternoon and we've got about two hours of sunlight left – you up for a low-level on the way back?"

"Is Griswold Beckett a lunatic?"

"He certainly is. He certainly is. Is that your way of saying yes?"

"Yes."

"Good! And what do you think about my plan, eh?"

"Let's talk later over a beer."

"Heh-heh, I thought so. Well, come on! Let's get airborne. I hate being on the ground."

We took off toward the water and banked hard right toward the Talamancas. Walt wanted the scenic route so we plotted a course through the center of the country and settled in at 300 feet. Even in Panama there was a lot left to see.

The List

1. One vicuña pullover

2. A case of Kunstman lager

3. Dirt from the collpa de Guacajayos

4. A stele (Jaguar Paw, from Copan)

5. Two Brazilian lottery tickets

6. A skull

7. A petroglyph

8. A pizote

9. A Monarch butterfly

10. A flute

11. Tagua nuts

12. A sisal

13. Wings

14. Warekena pitcher

15. A coat of arms

16. A Korubo war club

17. A rainstick

18. A coconut

19. The branch of a carob tree

20. A cayuca

21. The wheel of a paddleboat steamer

22. Tapir fishhooks

23. Lotus fiber sleeping mat

24. Maximón

25. The Sol of Antofogasta

26. One blue gentian

27. Vilcabamba's gold

Glossary

Albrook AB – Albrook Air Base, the second largest American air base in Panama. It sat on the east side of the Canal, right next to Panama City.

ADO – Assistant Director of Operations. The #3 officer in a squadron.

AOC – Air Operations Center

APU – Auxiliary Power Unit (a small jet engine that the C-27 used to get the main engines turning)

DEA – Drug Enforcement Agency

DNIF – Duties Not Involving Flying (meaning a pilot is too sick to fly but can be assigned to desk work)

DO – Director of Operations. The #2 officer in a squadron.

DZ – Drop Zone

FAIP – First Assignment Instructor Pilot

FOD – Foreign Object Damage

Group – The next level in the chain of command above a squadron. Above the Group is a Wing.

GPS – Global Positioning System

Howard AB – Howard Air Base, the main American air base in Panama. It sat on the west side of the Canal, away from the city and along the Pan-American Highway leading out into the countryside.

INS – Inertial navigation system

LZ – landing zone

NCO – Non-Commissioned Officers (sergeants)

OSI – Office of Special Investigations (the Air Force detectives who try to ferret out spies)

Soto Cano AB – an American air base in Honduras, about 800 miles from Panama City. It was used during the 1980s to support the contras in Nicaragua but by 1990 was almost a ghost town. A small Army detachment called Task Force Bravo was stationed there but except for the occasional cargo plane passing through, the runway and ramps were usually deserted.

TAS – Tactical Airlift Squadron

TDY – Temporary Duty (a short trip to a location other than one's normal air base)

Stan/Eval – Standardization and Evaluation Office (the senior pilots who give check rides to everyone else)

VVI – Vertical Velocity Indicator (a needle that points up or down to tell you how fast the plane is climbing or descending)

About the Author

Michael Bleriot is a military and civilian pilot. For several years he flew tactical airlift in Central and South America, supporting local militaries and U.S. forces in their attempts to limit the production and distribution of illegal drugs.

www.ingramcontent.com/pod-product-compliance
Lightning Source LLC
LaVergne TN
LVHW051547070426
835507LV00021B/2450